The Lives
of Spiders

The Lives
of Spiders

Dorothy Hinshaw Patent

HOLIDAY HOUSE · New York

To the spiders which hunt in my garden,
giving me the pleasure of watching them
as they rid my plants of unwelcome insects.

Library of Congress Cataloging in Publication Data

Patent, Dorothy Hinshaw.
  The lives of spiders.

  Bibliography: p.
  Includes index.
  SUMMARY: Describes the characteristics and habits
of spiders in general, as well as a number of
specific spiders.
    1. Spiders—Juvenile literature. [1. Spiders]
I. Title
QL 458.4.P37   595.4'4   80-14801
  ISBN 0-8234-0418-8

Contents

The golden-silk spider, Nephila clavipes, *can be recognized easily by the tufts of hairs on its legs. The body of this female spider resting in her web is about an inch long. Her tiny ¼-inch mate weights about 1/100 as much as she does.* CATHY CALLAHAN

One

The Misunderstood Spider

Wherever you live, you are familiar with spiders, for these adaptable little animals can make their homes in the heart of the city as well as in the lushest pastures and deepest woods. Perhaps you, like so many people, are afraid of them. Fear of spiders is so common that there is even a fancy name for it—arachniphobia, although the reasons for it are somewhat of a mystery. The overwhelming majority of spiders are harmless to people, with only a few especially poisonous kinds in the United States. Spiders are actually our helpers, for they eat vast quantities of harmful insects which might otherwise damage our crops or bother us in other ways. Perhaps people fear spiders because they appear unexpectedly in our homes and look so strange. Indeed, the spider's world is very different from ours. But that is part of what makes these little hunters and trappers so interesting. By peering into their lives, we can "see" Earth from a completely different viewpoint.

Spiders, Spiders Everywhere

If you think for a moment, you will realize that you have seen several kinds of spiders at different times. Just inside and around your home, a dozen or more kinds probably live. Altogether, there are over 30,000 known kinds of spiders, and it is believed there are as many as 120,000 others yet to be described and named.

Spiders live almost anywhere life can survive, from the slopes of Mt. Everest (up to 6,700 meters—22,000 feet) to the lowest, driest deserts. They thrive from the far south of Australia to the northern coast of Greenland, only 644 kilometers (403 miles) from the North Pole. As a matter of fact, at least 50 species inhabit that barren, misnamed land. Even when the temperature dips below freezing, some northern spiders remain active, spinning their webs in snow crevices to catch tiny insects which are also active in the cold.

While many spider species are at home in frozen lands, even more kinds spend their lives in the hot deserts of the world. Desert spiders usually avoid the heat by spending the daytime hours buried underground or hiding in the shade of desert plants. At night they come out, along with the other desert creatures, to feed and look for mates.

A few spiders can skim over the water's surface to grab drowning insects, and some dive below the surface to catch small fish. One European spider spends its entire life underwater, using its silk to trap an air bubble, a private "diving bell" containing vital oxygen. The seashore even has its share of spiders, which can tolerate the saltiness of the ocean.

One thing is sure—wherever insects can live, spiders are there to prey on them. Without insect food, most spiders would starve to death, although some spiders specialize in eating other spiders. Spiders are often found at great altitudes, floating on silken strands, but they eventually come down to earth. Scientists sampling the air find many spiders drifting about at 61 meters (201 feet), and occasionally come across them as far up as 3,050 meters (10,065 feet). Perhaps one reason spiders are found in so many places is this ability to travel long distances through the air, even though they lack wings.

Not only are spiders found just about everywhere, they are found in amazingly large numbers. Scientists have estimated that tens to hundreds of thousands of spiders make their homes in an acre of grassland. Some spin webs among the tufts of grass, while others wander about hunting for prey. Still others, which you will not see unless you look for them, live secluded lives among the fallen leaves and dead grass which cover the ground or live within the earth itself.

What Are Spiders?

You may have learned that spiders are not insects, but do you know why? Actually, insects are no more closely related to spiders than they are to shrimps and crabs. Hundreds of millions of years ago, some water-dwelling creatures, the ancestors of insects, began experimenting with life on land. Since that time, their descendants have evolved into the hundreds of thousands of insect species alive today. The ancestors of spiders, too, crept out of the water millions of years ago. But they were different from the insect ancestors. So insects and spiders have evolved completely separately into many land-living species.

Even so, there are some similarities between these two animal groups. Some of the similarities exist because both insects and spiders are members of the great group of related animals called the Phylum Arthropoda. Arthropods, as they are called, are the most numerous animals on Earth in terms of numbers of species. They are also among the most numerous in terms of numbers of individual animals. Other arthropods include crabs, shrimp, "sow bugs" (actually not bugs at all), centipedes, scorpions, ticks, and mites.

The name arthropod means "jointed legged." All arthropods have a hard outer body-covering which has joints in the legs so that they can be bent. The hard covering, called the "cuticle," is really the animal's skeleton, for the muscles are attached to it and pull against it to allow movement. This "exoskeleton" ("exo-" means outside) has several advantages over an inside ("endo-") skeleton such as we have. The exoskeleton protects the soft body organs of the animal from enemies; it is a built-in suit of armor. It also helps shield the animal from drying out.

But an exoskeleton also has disadvantages. It must become thicker the larger the animal. Arthropods never get to be very large, because a large animal would require an exoskeleton too heavy to move about. The exoskeleton also limits the growth of the animal. A spider or insect can get only so large inside its armor. When arthropods are growing, they must cast off the exoskeleton now and then, grow rapidly, and harden up a new suit of armor. Thus, rather than growing continuously, arthropods grow in very short spurts, during the time the new exoskeleton is still soft. Because the muscles pull against the hard skeleton to allow movement, an arthropod which has just shed is very weak and easy prey to enemies.

What Makes Spiders Different

Some of the differences between insects and spiders are easy to see, while others are less obvious. The insect body has three parts—the head, the thorax, and the abdomen. The spider has only two parts, the combined head and thorax, called the cephalothorax ("cehphalo-" means head in Greek), and the abdomen. Insects have six legs, while spiders have eight. If you look at the head of a spider and that of an insect with a magnifying glass, you can see some

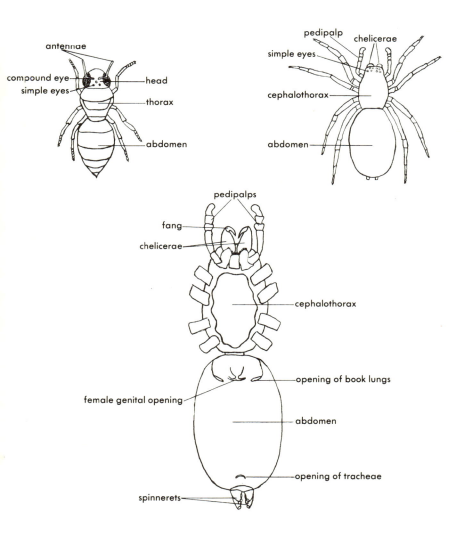

Spiders and insects have very different bodies. On the left is a bee with its wings removed; on the right is a spider. The insect has three body sections, antennae, compound and simple eyes, and six legs. The spider has two body sections, pedipalps, simple eyes, and eight legs. Below is a female spider with the legs removed, as seen from below. DRAWING BY THE AUTHOR.

other differences. All insects have a pair of antennae on the head which helps them sense the world around them. Spiders lack antennae, but they do have appendages in front. The first appendages on a spider's head are called chelicerae (pronounced key-lis'-er-ee). The tips of the chelicerae are the spider's fangs, which it uses to pierce the bodies of its prey. Most spiders use poison injected through tiny openings in the chelicerae to subdue their victims. Besides the chelicerae, spiders have another pair of appendages called pedipalps. Pedipalps are very similar to legs, only smaller and somewhat different in structure. Males and females use their pedipalps for different purposes, as we will see later.

If you examine the head of an insect such as a bee or a butterfly, you will see its large and impressive compound eyes. Each eye is made up of hundreds or thousands of tiny individual units. In addition to the compound eyes, many insects have other, simpler eyes as well. For example, the honeybee has three simple eyes on the top of its head in addition to its huge compound eyes. Spiders lack compound eyes completely. All their eyes—most spiders have eight of them—are simple eyes called ocelli.

Water animals often use gills to absorb oxygen from the water. But gills must be kept moist to function, so most land animals have evolved other ways of getting enough oxygen to meet their needs. There are both similarities and differences between the ways insects and spiders have solved the problem of extracting oxygen from the air. Insects have tiny air tubes called tracheae which penetrate the depths of the body, carrying air and with it oxygen to the tissues of the body. The original spider organs for obtaining oxygen are called "book lungs." The book lungs open by slits to the outside. Inside each book lung is a series of folds in the cuticle, like the pages of a book, which are held apart by tiny pillars.

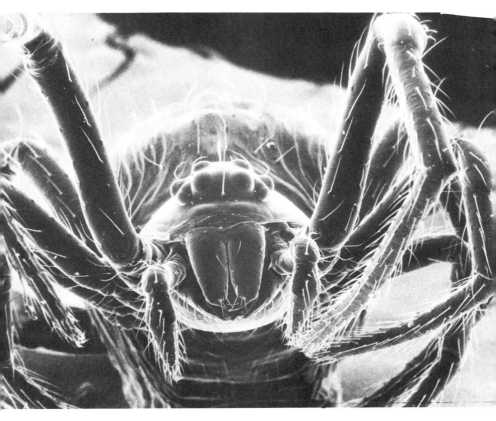

Spiders do not undergo a metamorphosis like butterflies. Even a young spiderling, like this black widow, has the typical spider body plan. On top of its head is a cluster of eight eyes. The chelicerae, with the fangs pointing towards each other, and the pedipalps reaching forward next to the chelicerae, can clearly be seen. DR. J. NORMAN GRIM, NORTHERN ARIZONA UNIVERSITY

Blood circulates in the spaces between the "pages" of each book. In this way, the blood gets up close to the air and can extract oxygen from it.

Some book lungs have over 100 leaves to them. Many spiders use book lungs as their only means of obtaining oxygen. Tarantulas and their relatives have two pairs of book lungs on the underside of the abdomen. But in most spiders, the back pair of book lungs are modified into tracheae similar to those of insects. Tracheae are most common in small spiders and in spiders which live in dry places. Some of these lack book lungs entirely. Tracheae can apparently extract oxygen from the air with less loss of water from the spider's body than can the book lungs.

Spider Relatives

While spiders are only distantly related to insects, they do have some familiar closer relatives. Spiders belong to the biological class Arachnida, along with scorpions, ticks, mites, and several groups of small, unfamiliar creatures which live hidden lives. All arachnids have chelicerae and pedipalps and a similar breathing system. All arachnids except for a few mites feed exclusively on liquid food, either sucking blood or releasing digestive enzymes from their mouths into their food so that it is partially digested before being sucked up .

Scorpions live over most of the world, except in colder regions. They are rather large for arachnids but are seldom seen because they spend the daytime hidden away in protected places. Scorpions have an undeserved reputation for being dangerously poisonous. In truth, scorpions found in North America do not have very strong venom, and because they are so shy, they rarely sting anyone. The main purpose of the scorpion stinger is to subdue prey animals. Scorpions have fascinating mating rituals in which the male grabs the pedipalps of the female and leads her about in a long, complicated dance.

Ticks are unpleasantly familiar creatures to people who spend time in the woods. Ticks are amazingly efficient parasites. A tick waits, perched quietly on a branch, until a warm-blooded animal passes beneath. Sensing the heat from the animal's body, the tick lets go and drops down onto its victim. There it wanders about for awhile, looking for a good place to sink its sharp chelicerae so it can suck blood. Ticks can be dangerous, for they carry several painful, sometimes fatal diseases of humans and animals.

Mites are more varied in their life styles than are other arachnids. Some mites live completely under water. Perhaps you have seen them in samples of pond water—little red or orange spheres with eight tiny legs paddling them along through the water. Other mites are plant pests, including the nasty spider mites which produce silk and attack house plants. Many mites are parasties of animals. Their small size enables them to live in some improbable places, such as inside the ears of moths or the eyelash follicles of humans.

The familiar daddy longlegs, or harvestman, is also an arachnid. These improbable-looking animals thrive in fields and gardens, walking delicately over leaves at night in search of such food as snails, worms, earwigs, and flies. "The study of harvestmen is the study of legs" is the motto of biologists interested in these creatures, for little but their legs is evident. While harvestmen do have two eyes on top of the head, one facing forward and its twin facing backwards, the legs are their tongues, nose, and probably their ears as well. The second pair of legs is especially important in sensing the environment. Although harvestmen drop their legs rather easily, loss of even one leg of the second pair is a real handicap for this unique creature.

In addition to these familiar arachnids, several groups of small, shy animals with names like false scorpions, whip-scorpions, micro whip-scorpions, and ricinulei are also in this surprisingly varied animal class. Most of these animals

Wind scorpions are large arachnids with powerful jaws, which usually live in deserts. This one is in a threat posture. M. H. MUMA

are little known even to biologists, for they live in the leaf litter which covers the forest floor or in other hidden habitats. Some are found in such great numbers when actively searched for that they must be of great importance in the biological scheme of things.

One final group of arachnids are the large and powerful wind-scorpions. These speedy hunters live mostly in desert areas and have perhaps the strongest jaws, relative to their size, in the entire animal kingdom. Some have jaws as long as their bodies. Wind-scorpions lack poison glands; their jaws are so strong and sharp that they can deliver a fatal bite to their prey without need for poison.

Two
The Spider's World

Trying to see the world from a spider's-eye view is much like imagining what life on another planet might be like. Even the phrase, "a spider's-eye view," trips us up. We take in the world around us primarily with our eyes. But most spiders use their eyes very little in their daily lives. While hearing is our second most important sense, spiders have no true ears and do not hear at all in the same sense that people do.

How do spiders keep in touch with their surroundings? The secret of a spider's senses is in its legs. While spiders do see with their eyes and can taste with at least some part of their mouths, they hear, feel, and smell with their legs. Spider legs are richly supplied with sense organs, from tiny microscopic hairs sensitive to movements of the air, to large, hollow, moveable spines which contain nerve endings. The hair-like setae on spider legs also contain sensory nerves.

Spider Senses

Because spider senses are so different from ours, it is often difficult to pin down the significance of some spider sense organs. Spiders and other arachnids have peculiar slits in the cuticle. Some of these slits occur singly or in loosely associated groups. Others are arranged in parallel fashion very close together. These groups of up to 30 slits are called lyriform organs. Most lyriform organs are located near the leg joints. There may be 3,000 slits on the body and legs of one spider. Inside each slit lies a thin membrane to which are attached the tiny endings of several nerve cells. Biologists have studied the slit organs for years, but no one has yet determined exactly how the spider perceives its surroundings through them. They react to mechanical stimulation—that is, anything that deforms the membrane covering the sensory cells sets off a nervous impulse. A great variety of stimuli can result in stimulation of the lyriform organs, such as vibration of the ground or web lines on which the spider rests; airborne sounds; or even movements of the spider's own body, including walking. Just how the spider sorts this all out to gain meaningful information about its surroundings is difficult for humans to understand.

The tarsal organs, through which spiders "taste," are less mysterious. These small, round holes in the exoskeleton are found on the end leg segment, called the tarsus. Each hole leads to a depression with a tiny projection inside. If a drop of water is placed on the tarsal organ of a front leg, the spider steps forward to drink. If the drop is placed on a hind leg, the spider turns around and drinks. Tarsal organs are also used to examine prey to determine their edibility.

Most spiders have eight eyes, but some are completely blind. Others have two, four, or six eyes. One minute spider living on the Panamanian jungle floor has only a single eye right in the middle of its head. Web-builders have rather weak eyes, for they use their exquisite sense of touch and sensitivity to vibrations to find out what is happening in the vital web. Hunting spiders, which do not rely on webs to capture prey, may have quite well-developed eyesight. They can see both shape and movement. While they have eight eyes, many of these spiders have one especially large pair in

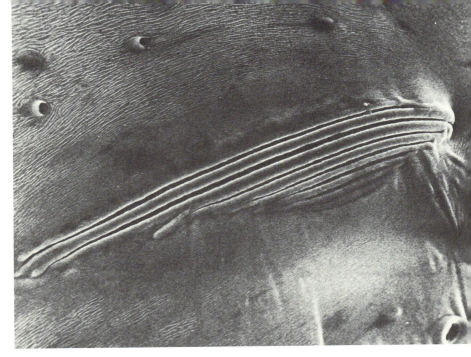

The lyriform organs of spiders consist of groups of tiny slits in the cuticle which lead to sensitive nerve cells. Lyriform organs are especially common near the leg joints, where they probably function in sensing body movements. PROF. DR. FRIEDRICH G. BARTH

front which is more complicated in structure than the others. The other six eyes are arranged over the head in such a way that they can detect movement anywhere around the spider. If one or more of these eyes perceives movement, the spider turns itself around so that the main eyes are aimed at the source of movement.

Getting Around

Besides being marvelous sense organs, spider legs also perform the down-to-earth function of getting their owner from place to place. Each kind of spider has legs well-adapted to its way of life. Some have long, skinny legs;

others have short, stubby ones. Web-builders are clumsy away from their silken homes, and hunters would easily become entangled in a web.

Spiders always have four pairs of legs, and each leg has a total of seven segments with joints between them. This gives their legs a lot more flexibility than ours, which have only two segments (the thigh and calf), in addition to the foot. At the tip of the spider tarsus (end leg segment) are two or three claws, depending on the spider species. Most web-builders have three claws, one of which is especially modified for hooking onto the web strands. The spider can move with confident ease through its web by catching the threads with these special claws.

Hunting spiders usually lack the third claw, for they run across plants or the ground instead of gliding delicately through a web. Hunters usually have shorter legs than web-builders. When a spider walks or runs, it moves its legs in a particular way. The first and third legs on one side step forward along with the second and fourth leg on the other side.

Living and Dying

Most spiders live what by human standards would be called short lives, a year or less. Most familiar spiders probably belong to this group. They hatch, grow up, reproduce, and die within a few short months. Some spiders spend the winter in protected places as full-grown adults. Such spiders inhabit the spring meadows in large numbers, spinning their webs and seeking their mates. Some wandering spiders, too, overwinter as adults and wander about in the springtime sunshine, hunting for food and mates. Soon the males of such species are dead and gone, while the females are busy spinning their egg sacs.

Other spiders spend the winter within protected egg sacs, hatching as tiny spiderlings in the springtime. These spiders grow to adulthood over the summer, mate in the fall, and leave their egg sacs in sheltered places to spend the winter. Thus, even though most spiders live a year or less, there are always adults of one kind or another around as well as growing young ones.

Male spiders always live shorter lives than the females. One scientist who kept black widows in his laboratory found that male black widows mature in an average of 70 days and live only about 100 days, while females mature in 90 days and survive for around 271 days. While one female lived a long life of 550 days, the most a male could manage to survive was 160 days. Even the male of the long-lived tarantulas cannot come near to matching the female in longevity. Most tarantulas become mature when about 10 to 12 years old; males die within a year of that time, while females can live on for another 10 or more years.

Molting and Growing

As we have seen, spiders must molt in order to grow. The old, too-small exoskeleton must be shed and replaced by a new, enlarged model. Small spiders reach maturity in as few as four or five molts. One very small spider, only pin-head size when full grown, becomes adult in only two molts. Medium-sized spiders must molt seven or eight times, while large ones do so more than ten times. While most spiders stop molting when they reach their adult size and sexual maturity, female tarantulas continue to molt even when grown and may molt a total of thirty or forty times.

Most spiders seek a protected place to molt, but web-builders may just hang quietly from the center of the web while shedding the old skin. The old exoskeleton splits down the middle of the back and is slowly worked over the body. The trickiest part of molting is pulling out the long legs, for they can get trapped inside the old skin, making the spider unable to free itself. Bit by bit, the spider pulls its soft legs out of the old covering, bending them back and forth to keep the joints flexible.

Many spiders die during molting, some because they cannot pull themselves out and others because they are attacked while relatively helpless. Creatures such as sowbugs, mealworms, and crickets, which otherwise are not serious spider enemies, may successfully attack a molting spider Their normal enemies, such as birds, also find them easier prey at this time.

All the spider's growth must take place while the pale new cuticle is still soft, before it hardens and darkens. Growth begins while the legs are being pulled out of the old exoskeleton. The legs of some spiders grow remarkably in length during the molt. The body, too, must increase in diameter during the molt. Extra water taken up by the spider's body allows it to increase in size rapidly.

The larger the spider, the longer it takes to molt. A spiderling may complete the whole process, from suspending itself in the web to lengthening its legs in only a half hour, with the actual molting taking less than five minutes. But a tarantula may lie helplessly on its back, working its old cuticle off gradually, for hours. Most spiders, however, take about two hours to molt.

Waiters and Hunters

All spiders live by attacking and eating animal prey, mostly insects. But, depending on the kind of spider, one of two very different strategies is used to obtain that prey. The familiar web-builders, along with such others as trap-door and crab spiders, use the sit-and-wait method. Web-builders construct a trap into which prey blunders. Trap-door spiders wait patiently in ambush, pouncing on whatever comes by their burrows. The familiar white or yellow crab spiders of the garden wait in ambush at a spot, such as on a flower, which is attractive to insects.

Other spiders actively search for food. Wolf and jumping spiders belong to this group. You have probably seen small jumping spiders walking on your windows or walls, searching for insects. Once I watched a determined little hunter stalking an ant along a window. The only trouble was, the ant was on the other side of the glass. The spider kept turning in the same direction as the ant, following it all over the window. It did not give up, even though it could never get to its intended prey.

Both ways of capturing prey have advantages and disadvantages. The spider which lies in wait uses up very little energy in the process, so it needs little nourishment to survive and even grow. One fly a week may be plenty of food for a small web-builder. When web-building spiders are starved, they use up even less energy, because their metabolic rate (a measure of how much energy an animal uses) drops 30 to 40 percent. They can survive long periods—some as long as 2½ years—without food.

One disadvantage of letting the prey come to the spider is that the spider has no way of controlling what it eats. It can only choose from what lands in its web or happens to wander by. Such spiders usually are not especially particular about what they eat. Although they may now and then reject some insect which enters the web, most such spiders will feed on any creature of appropriate size which comes along. But if a spider builds its web in an inappropriate place where few insects venture, it must either starve or move on to a better location.

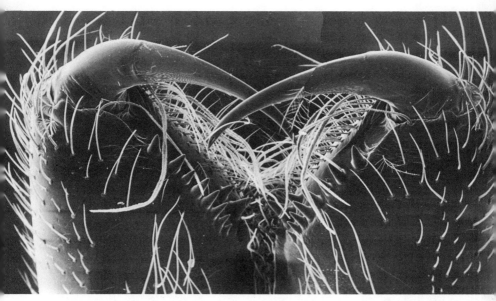

The spider's chelicerae are superb weapons for overpowering prey. The sharply pointed fangs have openings near the tips, which can be seen here, for injecting poison. Tooth-like spines on the inner edges of the chelicerae help it hold onto the prey securely. DR. R. F. FOELIX

The wandering hunters can pick and choose their food more easily than the waiters. But in the process of wandering about, they use up more energy and are perhaps easier prey themselves to other hunters. Wandering spiders do not have the assistance of an entangling web in the capture of their prey either. They must be able to subdue their victims quickly by grabbing them and injecting poison.

A Liquid Diet

All spiders, however, be they hunters or waiters, attack and consume their food by the same methods. The spiders' chelicerae have two segments. In the vast majority of spiders, the first segment, attached to the cephalothroax, contains poison glands. Sometimes the poison glands are so large that they extend back into the cephalothroax as well. Ducts from the glands pass out into the second segments, the fangs. The fangs are hollow and pointed, with small openings at their tips for the poison glands. In the tarantulas and their relatives, considered to be more primitive spiders, the chelicerae swing forward and backward. In order to attack prey, these spiders must rear up on their back legs. Other spiders move their chelicerae from side to side so they can separate them and bring them together, closing like pincers.

After injecting its poison, the spider releases digestive enzymes which reduce the prey to a liquid which can be sucked through the small spider mouth. Some spiders work the prey about, crushing it between their strong, toothed chelicerae as well as bathing it with enzymes. Other spiders merely wait until the enzymes have liquefied the insides of the hapless victim before sucking it up. Strong muscles attached to the stomach contract, enlarging the stomach and pulling in the liquid food.

Three
Spinners and Weavers

Ask any spider specialist for the secret of spider success and his immediate answer will be "silk." While a few other creatures make silk and use it for one purpose or another, only spiders have exploited this versatile and useful substance to its full potential. All spiders make silk, and it is important to the survival of almost all of them, including hunting spiders, which do not build webs. All spiders have at least three different kinds of glands producing silk, and some have as many as five different kinds. Spiders spin out their silken lines through small projections on the abdomen called spinnerets. A typical spider has three pairs of spinnerets, each of which is covered with hundreds of tiny holes through which the liquid silk comes out. When the silk hits the air it hardens, the thickness and strength of the thread being determined by how fast the spider lets out the thread. Spider silk may be as thin as a millionth of an inch across, and it can be stronger than steel.

Silk enters into every spider activity, from transportation and communication to prey-capture and predator-avoidance. The most fundamental thread for just about all spiders is the ever-present dragline, a strong double strand which is constantly let out wherever the spider goes. At intervals the dragline is glued down so that it is always safely an-

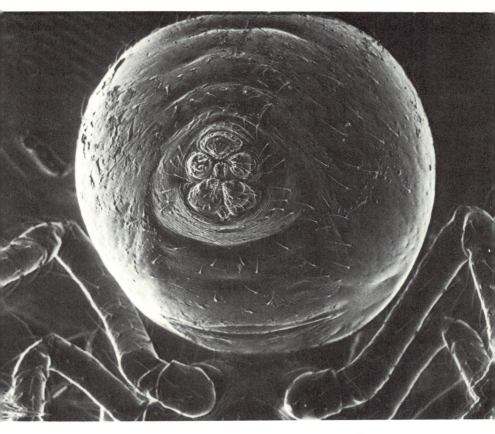

The spinnerets of a black widow form a compact bundle near the rear of the abdomen, as can be seen on this young spiderling.
DR. J. NORMAN GRIM, NORTHERN ARIZONA UNIVERSITY

chored. If a spider is threatened, it can immediately let go and drop down, disappearing magically while safely held suspended until danger passes. Most of us have had the somewhat alarming experience of having a suspended spider suddenly appear in front of our eyes as if it came from no-where. The dragline also lets the spider know where it has

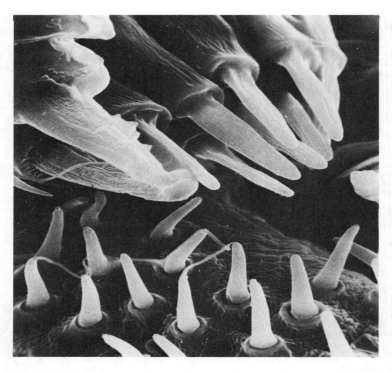

The spinnerets are really very complex structures, each with various spigots through which silk flows. This high-power photograph shows the different spigots of the front and middle spinnerets of an orb weaver. Strands of silk can be seen emerging from some of the spigots. DR. R. F. FOELIX

been and can be used to find the way back home. If you look at an unwashed window of a house in the country, you may see hundreds of dragline strands, left by passing spiders, gleaming in the sunlight.

Molding Silk

The silk-making apparatus of spiders is incredibly complex. At least seven kinds of silk glands are found in spiders, each producing a particular type of silk. From one to four pairs of spinnerets are connected to these glands by various-size tubes, allowing a great variety of silk to be produced. Most strands appear to have at least two separate threads, and as many as five pairs of fibers may be found in some web-mooring threads. One type of gland produces silk used in wrapping prey, another is used in making the attachment disks which hold down draglines, and still another produces the draglines themselves. All spiders have these three kinds of glands. Females of many spider species also have other glands making special egg-sac silk, while still other glands in some web-builders make sticky droplets used to trap prey.

The spinnerets as well as the silk glands vary from one kind of spider to another. Different spinneret pores are used for different kinds of silk. Attachment-disk silk comes out of tiny holes in the tips of the front pair of spinnerets, while the thick band of silk used to wrap prey emerges from similar tiny pores in the back spinnerets. Larger tubes on the spinnerets are used for laying down the dragline, for making the egg sac, and for depositing the sticky covering of the capture threads.

One group of spiders has still another silk-making tool. Called the cribellum, this flat plate in front of the spinnerets is studded with minute holes and produces a tangle of very fine threads used to trap prey. These spiders have special combs of tiny teeth on their hind pair of legs which they use to pull out and lay down the threads from the cribellum.

Flying Away

Spiders use silken kites to travel to new homesites. Within minutes or days after emerging from the egg sac, the tiny young spiderling walks up to the top of a grass stalk or leaf, crouches down, lifts up its abdomen, and releases a few silken lines which are pulled out by the wind. Because the tiny spider is so light, these fine strands provide enough lift to carry it away on the breeze to a new home. Spiders traveling on the wind are said to be ballooning. When the spiderling lands, it may find itself in a favorable site and settle down. But if it lands in a less desirable spot, all it has to do is balloon away again and again until it finds a suitable homesite.

During spring and fall, the air may glisten from the thousands and thousands of strands which carry spiderlings about. This "gossamer" was often a puzzle to ancient peoples, who often did not realize its source. Spiders have landed on ships 320 kilometers (200 miles) out to sea, so these silky threads can carry them long distances. While ballooning effectively spreads out the baby spiders and allows them to find new homes, it also results in the death of many unfortunate young ones which land on the water or in unfavorable places. The advantages of spreading out, however, must outweigh the disadvantages, for almost every spider family has members which spread themselves out in this way. Even the adults of some small species may fly off to make their homes in new territory.

The Indonesian island of Krakatoa provides a dramatic example of how effective ballooning is. In August of 1883, two-thirds of the island was blown away by a terrific volcanic explosion, and all life there was extinguished. A visitor who stopped at Krakatoa nine months after the disaster found only one microscopically small spider and not a single blade of grass. Forty-eight years later, the island was repopulated by both plants and animals, including more than ninety different spider species. All but three of these were kinds which could have arrived by ballooning. The other three were all found only around the temporary huts imported by scientists studying the volcano. The nearest land is a very small island 16 kilometers (10 miles) away; other land is 40 kilometers (25 miles) distant.

Building Webs

Spiders and webs are so connected in our minds that it seems strange that only about half of all known spiders actually spin webs. The rest use different ways of capturing their prey. But among web-spinners there is quite a variety of web types, each adapted to the circumstances under which its owner must live. The web actually performs several functions for its owner. It is an extension of the spider's senses; by feeling the vibrations of its threads, the spider can be aware of the nearness of either enemy or prey.

The web can protect the spider from its enemies by entangling them or slowing their approach. It can intercept prey insects over a much larger area than the spider could without itself moving about, and it can entrap that prey or place it at a distinct disadvantage by tripping or entangling it. Many webs are obvious in the morning when covered with dew, but usually they are almost invisible to us even in broad daylight. Many webs rarely come to human attention, for they are built in hidden places such as under rocks, or are constructed during the night and taken down before dawn.

Webs come in a variety of shapes and sizes, with each species making a particular kind of web. The spider inherits the ability to make the right kind of web, for young spiders with no previous experience build just the right kind without practice. Some spiders, such as black widows and many house spiders, make tangled webs with no apparent order to them. Other species make "sheet webs" to capture flying insects. A maze of trip lines is built over a flat mat of silk. When a flying insect hits a trip line, it falls on the silken mat, which acts much like a trampoline or aerial safety net. While the insect is trying to get on its feet, the spider rushes up to it, often from the underside of the mat, and bites it.

The most famous spider webs are the orbs, made by spiders of several different families. This most efficient type of web has probably evolved separately at least twice. The orb web is composed of a framework of strong lines within which radial strands connect the center of the web with the framework. A spiral thread which ensnares the prey is anchored to the radial lines. One group of orb weavers uses a sticky liquid placed in tiny blobs along the spiral to capture prey, while others make the spiral from the tangled, fuzzy silk of the cribellum.

Packaging the Meal

Once a spider has captured an insect in its web, it wraps it in silk, making it helpless. Some spiders bite their prey before wrapping it, while others wrap before biting. But whichever technique the spider uses, wrapping its prey in silk has several advantages. Wrapping first of all immobilizes the prey so that it can neither escape nor defend itself. Then the spider can bite and feed at its own leisure. If another insect should strike the web while the spider is feeding, the spider can dash off to attack and return later to feed further. Wrapping also covers any dangerous spines or other protective devices of prey animals. Spiders have been known to wrap up animals much larger than themselves and hoist them up into their webs, using the threads like a block-and-tackle mechanism. Wrapped prey can be moved to a corner of the web for later feeding, if prey is abundant at times and scarce at other times.

Egg Sacs

Another important use for silk is the building of egg sacs. Just like the spider Charlotte, the heroine of E. B. White's story, *Charlotte's Web*, most female spiders make their egg sacs as one of their last living acts and die before the young hatch. The egg sac is often made from several kinds of silk, fluffy silk surrounding and cushioning the eggs inside, and strong, tangled silk providing a protective coating. Often the egg sac silk is colored a delicate yellow or pink. Some spiders mix in bits of sand, plants, or prey-remains into the outer layer. This may provide effective camouflage.

Egg-sac silk is different from other silk. It is never sticky and is less flexible than dragline silk. Some egg sacs have a shiny outer layer which may be different in origin from the rest or may be laid down in a special way. Biologists have found that egg sacs do not appear to protect the eggs from changes in temperature, but they may help discourage predators and parasites from tackling their tangled mass of threads.

Four

The Not-So-Terrible Tarantulas and Their Kin

The word "tarantula" has an alarming sound to it. Most people, when they hear it, imagine a very large, hairy, vicious, and deady poisonous spider which they would prefer to avoid at all cost. This image is so deeply ingrained that information to the contrary is often ignored or disbelieved. The truth is that the tarantulas which live in the United States are shy, peaceful creatures which bite only if greatly provoked. Their venom has virtually no effect on humans; a tarantula bite is no more painful or dangerous than any other minor puncture wound. As a matter of fact, the peaceful nature of this misunderstood creature, its beauty, its interesting habits, and its long life, have made it a favorite pet with hundreds of Americans. So many people desire to have pet tarantulas that some biologists worry about the decline of populations in the wild.

Spiders are divided into two distinct groups by biologists. Tarantulas, trap-door spiders, purse-web spiders, and some others are put together in the group referred to as the Mygalomorphae (Some call this group the Orthognatha). For convenience, they will be referred to as mygales here. These spiders are less specialized than the so-called "true spiders," the Araneomorphae. Megales tend to be large, but range from tiny funnel and sheet web-builders only a third of a centimeter (⅛ inch) long, to tropical tarantulas 8¾ centimeters (3½ inches) in body length. Mygales have four book lungs each, which is considered a "primitive" trait by scientists. Their chelicerae are also considered to be "primitive," for they can only be moved forward and backward, not from side to side. In order to attack their prey, these spiders must swing the chelicerae forward in front and raise up the body, stabbing downward to imbed the parallel fangs into the victim. Because most mygales are large and strong, they do not need large quantities of powerful venom to subdue their prey. Their poison glands are restricted to the chelicerae and do not extend into the body like those of some other spiders.

Most mygales live in warm places. Only one sort lives in the British Isles, while many different species inhabit the American deserts and the South American forests. Africa, India, Australia, Sri Lanka, and New Guinea have their share, too.

Tarantulas

About 30 species of tarantulas live in the United States. Most are found in the dry areas of the southwest. These shy spiders spend the daylight hours in their burrows, which are often made under large rocks. When the spider is at home, a thin layer of silk covers the entrance to the burrow. When darkness descends, the spider comes out of its home to hunt, searching for insects. While our female tarantulas may live to be over 20 years old, they rarely wander more than a few meters from their burrows, dashing back with remarkable speed if disturbed.

Tropical tarantulas may be quite different from our native species. They are often larger and may be quite colorful, with red and brown stripes on their legs or other attractive markings. Hollywood films may feature giant tarantulas from time to time, but in real life none get quite as big as films would make you believe. The largest tarantulas, however, are large enough to alarm many people. Tarantulas weighing as much as 8½ grams (3 ounces) with a leg span of 25 centimeters (10 inches) have been found. The jungles of South America house the largest tarantulas.

While species living in the United States are generally burrowers, some jungle tarantulas are most at home in the trees, climbing up using special sticky pads on their tarsae and nesting above ground. Some of these powerful giants even prey on birds. Hobbyists who keep pet tarantulas sometimes report that their tropical pets show little or no interest in crickets or meal worms and perk up only if fish, frogs, or other vertebrate prey are offered as food. Some of these tropical tarantulas can even kill and eat small poisonous snakes. Strangely enough, not much is known about just how poisonous these spiders are to humans, although it seems that even the big jungle species are quite harmless aside from the pain of the bite.

In addition to their powerful fangs, tarantulas have an unusual weapon which may account for the belief that they are poisonous. Many species have a patch of hairs on the top of the abdomen which break off easily. These hairs have tiny hooks and barbs which catch in the skin of small mammals that may make the mistake of attacking the spider. When threatened, many tarantulas rub the top of the abdomen with the last pair of legs and fling a cloud of irritating hairs at the enemy. People with pet tarantulas need be more careful of these hairs than of a possible bite, for the hairs can cause quite an uncomfortable rash. Some people develop an increasing sensitivity, too, if they are exposed to them several times.

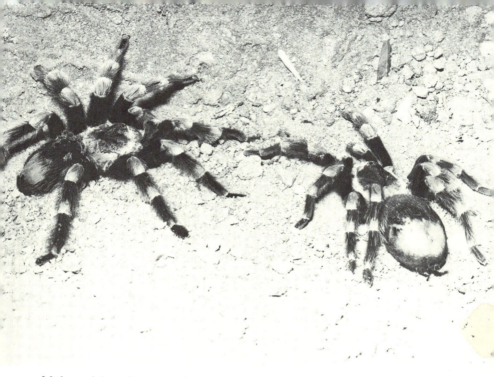

Male and female tarantulas are similar in size. The male Mexican red-leg on the left has a smaller abdomen than the female on the right. Both spiders have bare patches on their abdomens. The irritating hairs on the abdomen are used in defense.
R. HOWARD HUNT

The Tarantula Family

Most species of tarantulas found in the United States become sexually mature when they are about 10 years old. After the final molt, a complete change comes over the male spider. He has spent his whole life in and around one burrow; now he must wander until he finds a mate. The female tarantula may produce a chemical which attracts the male; this has not been actually proved, but it seems likely.

After locating the female's burrow, the male spider vibrates his third pair of legs, causing gentle vibration of the ground as signals to the female. If she is interested, she will tap her front legs in response. After the brief mating (described later), the male usually gets away, but sometimes may end up as a meal for his mate. In any case, the male will die soon, for he does not live more than a year after becoming sexually mature.

The female weaves a careful egg sac for her eggs, which she keeps with her in the burrow. After the young spiders hatch, they stay with her for days or sometimes weeks. Eventually, they wander off to build their own tidy burrows in which they enlarge gradually as they molt and grow into adulthood.

Trap-Door Spiders

There is something appealing about the trap-door spider, an animal which builds itself a soft silken tunnel and caps it with a hinged door. Trap-door spiders have among the most restricted lives of all spiders, for they spend their entire lives inside their cozy tubes, reaching out only far enough to grab unsuspecting passersby. The effects of sun, wind, and rain are all cushioned by the protected tube so that the spider experiences a very limited range of stimuli.

Three kinds of trap-door nests are made by these various spiders. One type has a thick, cork-like door with carefully beveled edges, which fits perfectly into the top of the tube. The door is made of several layers of silk, mixed in with dirt. It is perfectly camouflaged, lying even with the surrounding soil when closed. This cork-like door closes by itself from its own weight, so its owner must hold it ajar while waiting for passing victims. The tube is dug with the help of short, strong spines on the spider's front legs which aid in scraping the soil. The nest is only about 12 to 20 centimeters (5 to 8 inches) long and has about the same diameter throughout. The plump spider with its short legs

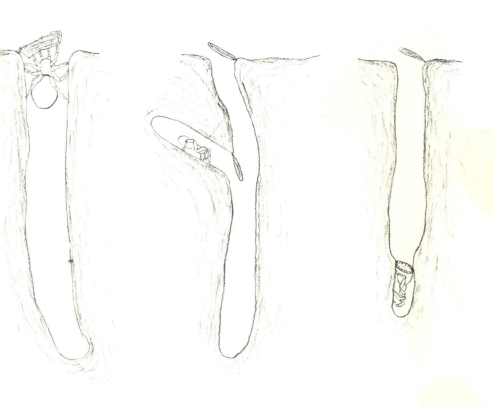

Spiders make different sorts of trap-door tunnels. On the left is a typical trap-door spider tunnel with a thick door made from silk and soil. The spider grabs onto the door and the sides of its burrow with its claws if disturbed and hangs on tightly. In the middle is a trap-door nest with a side tunnel. The door is a thin silk wafer. The spider can run into the side tunnel if frightened and close the inside door. The tunnel on the right also has a wafer-thin door. When the spider is frightened, it runs down into the narrow bottom of the tunnel and uses its armored abdomen to close off the tunnel. DRAWING BY THE AUTHOR.

can turn around easily within its protected home. If the spider is alarmed, it quickly closes the door and grabs onto it with its chelicerae and claws while bracing its legs against the sides of the burrow. The spider hangs on so tightly that it is difficult even for a person prying with a knife to open up the door.

One intriguing type of trap-door nest has a branched tunnel. The door on this type of nest is wafer-thin and is made up only of silk, with no dirt mixed in. Although it may be camouflaged with bits of moss or debris, it is too flimsy to act as much of a barrier to a determined predator such as a wasp. In addition to the main tunnel, this type of nest has a side branch as well with its own thin silken door. The door is hinged on top in such a way that it can be used to close off either the main tunnel or the side branch.

Unfortunately, little is known about how the spiders actually utilize their side tunnels. One biologist studied a species which built its nest near ant hills. He believed that ants which fell into the nest through the open door were then trapped inside when the spider swung the second door upward, closing off any route of escape. Other biologists think the side tunnel allows the spider to escape from an invading wasp. As the wasp rushes down the main tunnel, the spider slips quietly into the side tunnel, closing the door behind it. The wasp would thus search the main tube and find no one at home, leaving without finding the hidden spider.

Still another type of trap-door spider has a simple tunnel with no side branch and a wafer-thin door. This might seem like a poor sort of home for a creature with enemies like stinging wasps, but this spider has a special trick. The back of its abdomen is flattened and thickened into a tough shield. The nest narrows down near the bottom instead of being the same diameter throughout. When alarmed, the spider rushes down the tunnel head first until its armored abdomen neatly closes off the tube. Once thus stuck in, the spider holds on for dear life with its claws. The abdominal armor is so thick that the spider is well protected in this position.

Purse-Web Spiders

The purse-web spiders are a remarkable group of my-gales. They live in our southeastern states, although they sometimes are found as far north as Connecticut and Rhode Island. One species is also found in Great Britain. These spiders have developed a life style which takes advantage of the up-and-down movement of the chelicerae. They live in silken tubes like the trap-door spiders, only the tubes do not end at the soil surface. They extend up above the ground, often attached to tree trunks. At the top of the tube is a tiny hole. The tube also goes down quite a distance into the ground. The spider lives within this tube its whole life, a prisoner in its self-made dungeon. While building the tube, the spider remains inside at all times, spinning layer upon layer of silk and digging up bits of soil from the bottom of the nest which are carried above ground, pressed through the silk, and attached to the outside wall, making an even camouflaging coating on the outside. Extra dirt is formed into little balls which are pushed out through the tiny hole at the top. The spider waits just below ground level for insects to stray across the surface of its tube. The instant an insect ventures onto the tube, the spider senses the vibrations and rushes up. It thrusts its fangs through the silken wall of the nest, penetrating or enclosing the body of the prey instantly. The spider hangs onto it until it quiets down and then pulls it through a tear in the silk made by sharp teeth on the chelicerae. After feeding, the tidy spider carries the remains up to the top and throws them out through the hole. When she must pass feces, she backs up to the hole and releases the milky liquid forceably through the opening so that it lands safely away from her home.

Five
Traps and Snares

Some mygales build webs which trap prey, but the most accomplished web-builders by far are found among the "true" spiders. The name true spiders is an unfortunate one, since it implies that there is something false or unspiderlike about tarantulas and trap-door spiders. True spiders have developed many different ways of using silk to capture prey, some of them quite amazing. Webs range in organization from the senseless tangle of the comb-footed spiders (Theriidae), such as the black widow, to the elegant orbs of garden spiders and others. Webs range in size and complexity from the single line trap of the tropical Miagrammopes to the huge, communal webs of many social spiders, which may be dense and extensive enough to smother the trees upon which they are spun.

The Expert Entanglers

Spiders with the flat spinning plate called the cribellum use its finely tufted threads in various ways. The cribellum is studded with from 400 to 40,000 tiny spigots through which its extremely fine, woolly threads (only .0000125 millimeters; .00000049 inches in diameter) are released. All these spiders have a special row of tiny teeth, called the calamistrum, along one edge of the back legs, which is used to comb out the liquid silk from the cribellum, rather like a teasing comb used on human hair. These spiders use various techniques to comb out the cribellar silk. The woolly strands from the cribellum are called hackled bands. The typical tangled-web weaver named Amaurobius has a cribellum divided into two sides so that two bands of silk are produced at once. As it spins, Amaurobius rests the tip of one hind leg against the opposite hind leg while it rubs the calamistrum against the cribellum. The tangled ribbons from the cribellum are hooked onto ordinary silk lines from a pair of spinnerets as they are produced. After spinning for awhile, the spider shifts its legs and uses the calamistrum on the other hind leg. The resulting bluish silk strands are woven into a tangled web usually found under stones, in cracks in rocks, or around old stumps.

A common house spider, especially in the southern states, is Filistata. This spider puts much more effort into its web than does Amaurobius. First the spider lays down lines of ordinary dry silk in a radial pattern. Then it goes back and attaches threads from the cribellum. The cribellar threads are quite rough and have many tiny loops which easily entangle the spines of the feet and bodies of unsuspecting insects which may land on it.

Some hackled band weavers use remarkable methods to capture prey. The mostly tropical ogre-faced spiders are weird beasts with one very large pair of eyes pointing forward rather like headlights on a car. Their other eyes are quite small. One species, named *Dinopis spinosus*, lives in some parts of the southern United States, including Florida. This spider is usually thought to be rare, but it may be common in some areas. Because it is completely inactive in the daytime and resembles a bit of twig or dried leaf when resting, Dinopis can easily be overlooked. At sundown, however, Dinopis comes alive. She spins a framework of dry threads, across which are stretched many thick bands of tangled threads from the cribellum. The entire web is about the size of a postage stamp. Then the spider does a strange thing. Instead of waiting for passing insects to become entangled, the spider hooks her four front legs into the web. She holds the catching part between her legs as she hangs head downward, grabbing onto the dry lines with her hind legs. The spider hangs still until a flying insect approaches. Then she suddenly flings out her front legs, spreading them wide and enlarging the web to several times its original size. While the "net" is probably not actually thrown over the victim, it is held in the path of the prey, which flies right into it.

Dinopis longpipes, which lives in Panama, makes a similar trapping web. But this sharp-eyed spider positions itself above the trails of leaf-cutter ants, daubing its sticky net down onto the ants as they march by. These spiders will strike out at shadows passing beneath their nets, and their headlight eyes seem especially suited to seeing in very dim light.

Another sort of small web is made by Hyptiotes, the triangle spider. Hyptiotes is found in most of our states, but because of its small size (2 to 4 mm; less than $\frac{1}{10}$ to $\frac{2}{10}$ inch) it is not often noticed. The web of this little spider is like a wedge taken out of an orb. It has a Y-shaped framework with a total of 4 radii held together by cross lines of hackled bands. The stem of the Y is attached to a twig, and the spider positions herself along this line. She pulls on the anchoring line until the web is taut, holding the slack over her body. When an unsuspecting insect flies into the web. Hyptiotes quickly releases the slack, loosening the web suddenly so that it even more effectively ensnares the prey. If the victim is large and is struggling hard, the spider may tighten and snap the line several times, thoroughly entangling the insect. Then the spider climbs up to it, turns her back, and wraps it completely up with thick, bluish webbing. Unlike most spiders, Hyptiotes lacks poison glands, relying completely on the effectiveness of its entangling web and heavy swathing wrapper to keep the prey helpless.

The tropical stick spiders (Miagrammopes) make what is possibly the most improbable web of all. These skinny, long-legged brown spiders are covered with tiny grayish hairs and look very much like small sticks. Some stick spiders span open spaces in the forest with their one-line webs which may extend more than 120 centimeters (4 feet) from twig to twig. The midsection of the line, about 45 centimeters (18 inches), consists of a thick hackled band. After laying out her line, the stick spider pulls it taut as she positions herself near one of the mooring twigs. Because of her protective coloration and shape, she looks like nothing more than an extension of the twig. When an insect is foolish enough to think the line is a fine place to alight, the spider lets out a bit of the line quickly so that it jerks, ensnaring the victim more thoroughly. The stick spider then springs into action, rushing out to cover the victim with thick, bluish silk until it is helpless. She then cuts it out of the line, repairs the damage, and returns to her place with her meal.

Maze Webs

A great variety of web types is also made by spiders without a cribellum (called "ecribellate" spiders; "e" means without). Quite a few make simple maze webs which lack any sort of special catching threads. The common cellar spider (*Pholcus phalangiodes*) lives in basements and other dark places almost everywhere in the world. The body of this pale, whitish spider is only a little over ½ centimeter (¼ inch) long, but its legs measure 5 centimeters (2 inches). Because of its long, skinny legs, Pholcus is often confused with the harvestman. But the cellar spider is a true spider, spinning its irregular tangled cobweb along the ceilings and walls of cellars. When an insect hits the web, Pholcus shakes its web violently, entangling the prey further. It then attacks the victim, twisting it around and covering its body with silk before devouring it.

Many spiders which commonly inhabit houses belong to the family of comb-footed spiders (Theridiidae). Most comb-footed spiders prefer living in dark places and come out mostly at night. Their small eyes are gathered together in a close group near the front of the head. Their name comes from the combs of spines on the tarsi of the fourth pair of legs. These curved and toothed spines are used to throw silk over the prey. Instead of approaching their victims straight on, the comb-footed spiders back up to them and pull silk out from the spinnerets, tossing it onto the prey to entangle it further before attacking.

While some of these spiders make a simple maze web, many produce a snare with a more complex design. Often a sheet of closely woven threads is present under which the spider hides. Many comb-footed spiders, such as the notorious black widow, may build a funnel-shaped retreat. Some of these spiders put a lot of time and energy into making their nests. The European spider *Theridion saxatile* makes itself a nest in the middle of its maze of silk. Remains of prey, bits of dirt, and plant material may all be incorporated into this retreat. The spider lowers itself to the ground, selects a bit of sand, and attaches a thread to it. Then it climbs back into the nest with the building block attached to the thread. It uses one hind leg to hold onto the thread, half way between the sand and the spinnerets, to keep the load from swinging too wildly. When it reaches its nest, the spider turns around and grabs the grain with its front legs, pulling it up to the edge of the nest. It then care-

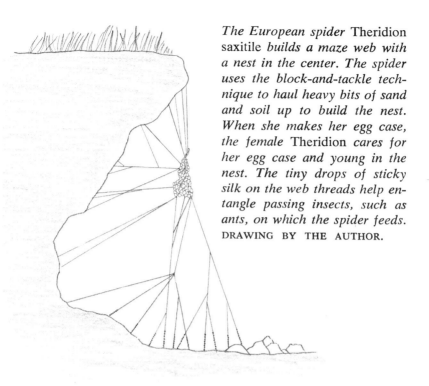

The European spider Theridion saxitile *builds a maze web with a nest in the center. The spider uses the block-and-tackle technique to haul heavy bits of sand and soil up to build the nest. When she makes her egg case, the female* Theridion *cares for her egg case and young in the nest. The tiny drops of sticky silk on the web threads help entangle passing insects, such as ants, on which the spider feeds.* DRAWING BY THE AUTHOR.

fully positions the bit of sand and spins a few strands of silk around it to hold it in place.

This ability to hoist heavy objects up by a "block-and-tackle" technique is also used in bringing prey into the nest. Many comb-footed spiders, such as Theridion, attach their webs to the ground by threads which have globs of sticky glue on them. Insects walking along the ground stumble into these threads and become entangled by the glue. The spider runs down its web and throws silk over the victim, making it helpless; then it bites and injects its venom. The prey may weigh many times as much as the spider. But the tiny trapper raises the victim, fastening it wtih many threads and gradually tightening and loosening key threads, until it rests several centimeters from the ground. Then the spider can settle down to feast for days.

The web of the bowl-and-doily spider has two sheets, one above the other. DR. HERBERT W. LEVI

Sheets and Domes

The most numerous spiders in temperate regions like the United States and Great Britain are the tiny sheet-web weavers (Linyphiidae). They usually spin their small but beautiful webs in the grass or very close to the ground, where people do not often notice them. The filmy dome spider (*Prolinyphia marginata*) is very common along paths and streams in shady, damp areas. Its delicately beautiful web consists of a filmy dome, about 7 to 12 centimeters (3 to 5 inches) across, surrounded by a maze of lines attached to nearby leaves and twigs. The spider stations herself under the dome center, where she waits for insects which hit the upper lines and fall upon the dome. If the prey gets too entangled in the upper lines, the spider may shake the web to bring it down onto the dome. There she bites it, pulls it through the webbing, ties it up with more silk, and feeds on it. Any rips in the dome are promptly repaired.

Many variations on the maze and sheet web exist. Some webs have one flat sheet surrounded by lines, while others have two sheets, one above the spider and one below it. The bowl-and-doily spider (*Frontinella communis*) makes a shallow bowl-shaped web filled with a maze of stopping threads. The spider hangs below this web, protected from enemies from below by a flat sheet web underneath her.

Quite a few spiders in this group live in caves. Some spin their sheet webs along the cave ceilings, while others live under the rocks on the cave floor. Many of these spiders have especially weak eyes, and some have lost their eyesight altogether.

Elegant Orbs

By far the most familiar and fascinating webs are those made by the orb web-weavers. The elegant perfection of these beautiful webs has inspired poets and scientists alike for ages. Thanks to the work of many biologists, we know a great deal about how these spiders put together their webs. Orb weavers are found on every continent except Antarctica. Most belong to one of two spider families. Strangely enough, one of these families (Uloboridae) belongs to the cribellate spiders, while the other (Araneidae) is an ecribellate family.

Most biologists believe that all ecribellate spiders are related to one another and that the cribellate spiders evolved separately. If this is true, then the ability to spin an orb web arose independently more than once. Some biologists find this hard to believe because the techniques used to build the web are identical in both families. They think that different groups of cribellate spiders gave rise to the various groups of ecribellate spiders and that the cribellum disappeared independently in each. If this were true, each ecribellate family would have different cribellate spiders as close relatives.

Although their webs have the same basic shape, orb weavers live a variety of life styles. Some are tiny and make their orbs down among the blades of grass, while others are very large and make meter-wide (about a yard) webs among high tree branches. Orb weavers live in the tropics and the northland, in meadows and in forests. Some put up their webs at dawn and trap day-flying insects; other hide until sunset and set up their snares only at dusk, using them to capture nighttime prey.

The orb web makes a superior trap for several reasons. Because it is positioned above the ground between plants, it can capture flying insects which would not encounter a maze and sheet web. Its near invisibility makes the orb web an especially effective snare. A minimum of silk is used to cover a maximum area, with the distance between capture threads determining the size range of prey. Little energy is used to build the web. The amount of energy in one or two flies is all it takes to construct a large orb which can trap 30 flies a day. Orb webs need only a few areas of attachment and can therefore be placed in a variety of locations, including spanning streams and forest paths. The radial construction of the orb gives it flexibility as well as strength and enables the spider to sense just where the prey is when it strikes the web.

Building a Masterpiece

Although the orb weaver may construct a new web each day, doing so is no easy job. Three or four different types of silk are used, along with two or three different kinds of glue. Many small tasks are involved in the project, too; in a typical orb with 39 radii and 35 spiral turns, the spiral must be attached to the radii at 1,225 separate points. Despite this complexity, it may take only a half hour to finish the job.

The very first step is to lay down a bridge line between two points, such as two tree branches. Depending on the circumstances, this line can be established in one of two ways. The spider may climb up to a high point and release a thin thread from its spinnerets. The wind then carries the thread away until it catches on another bit of plant. The spider then reels in any slack thread, pulling the bridge line tight. Any unsuccessful threads are reeled back in and eaten. If the web is being built close to the ground or up in the branches of a tree, the spider may fasten down one end of the bridge line and walk down, across, and back up a nearby branch or plant, pulling the line taut between the two anchoring points. Once the bridge line is set, the spider crosses it, letting out strong threads for reinforcement.

Next, the spider sets down the first three radii of the orb. It crosses the bridge line again, letting out a loose line as it goes. After anchoring the line at the far end, the spider crosses back along the sagging thread until it reaches the center. There it attaches a new thread and spins on down to another anchoring point. The web now consists of a Y-shaped framework with a bridge line across the top. The center of the "Y" will become the center of the web, and the three arms will become the principal radii of the web.

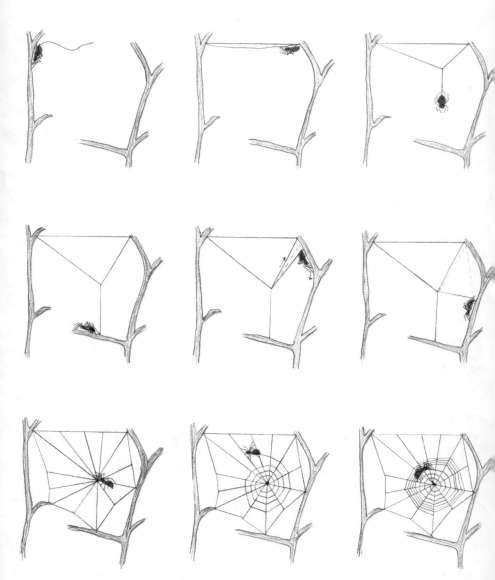

These diagrams show the steps in orb-web construction. First the spider lays down a bridge line which it strengthens with more threads. Then it attaches a strand near the middle of a bridge strand and reels out silk as it drops to another anchoring point.

Next, the spider fills in the rest of the radii, adding frame threads as necessary until a strong skeleton is formed. As it works, it may also reinforce the center area where the radial threads meet.

After all the radii are laid down, the spider builds a spiral, starting from the center of the web, using dry silk. This spiral is only a temporary, widely-spaced framework which holds the web together while the final, prey-catching spiral is built. After reaching the outer part of the web with the temporary spiral, the spider turns and travels back towards the center, laying down the catching spiral and cutting out the temporary one.

The catching spiral is different in the two main groups of orb weavers. The cribellate ones make it from two strands to which are attached fluffy fibers of silk from the cribellum. The ecribellate orb weavers lay down a line of two fibers covered with a sticky liquid. As the spider fastens down each segment of the spiral, it pulls on the thread, stretching it out like a rubber band. When released, the thread snaps back to its proper length, the sticky liquid now arranged in tiny droplets along the thread.

Usually the spider stops laying down the sticky spiral before reaching the center, leaving a free zone between the center and the catching thread. The center may be modi-

---

Then the spider lays down the other radii of its web. After the radii are all in place, the spider builds a temporary spiral from the center outwards. The temporary spiral holds the web together while the spider lays down the final, catching sticky spiral. As it attaches the sticky spiral, the spider rolls up the silk of the temporary spiral, which it later eats. Finally, many spiders modify the central hub of the web by adding strands or by biting out threads. DRAWING BY THE AUTHOR.

The web of Zygiella-x-notata *is an orb with one section left open. A signal thread crosses this open area. The spider waits hidden in the leaves, holding the far end of the thread. When an insect hits the web, the spider can feel the vibrations in the signal thread.* PETER N. WITT, M.D.

fied in various ways, depending on the species, and peculiar wide, zig-zag bands called stabilimenta may be added from the center outward. The function of the stabilimenta is debated, but they may serve to "tune" the web, perhaps equalizing the tension in the web or strengthening it where it is weak. Some biologists believe the stabilimenta function in some way as a defense against predators, perhaps as a net behind which the spider could hide if an enemy attacked.

Waiting for Food

Once the web is completed, the spider settles down to wait for prey. Many sit right in the center of the web with legs outstretched on the radii, ready to pick up vibrations made by potential victims. Others wait in the nearby foliage, connected to the center of the web by a thread which conducts the crucial vibrations. Some orb weavers leave out a segment of the spiral so that this signal thread can easily remain free from entanglement. When the spider senses vibrations in the web, it plucks at the radii to determine the exact location of the prey. Then it rushes out to attack.

Some orb weavers bite right away and then wrap the victim in silk, while others wrap before biting. The spider *Argiope argentata* reacts differently to different kinds of prey. If a fly hits the web, Argiope wraps it up before biting it. But when a moth comes along, the spider first gives it a long bite, injecting plenty of venom, before wrapping it. Moths do not stick very well in spider webs because their wing scales come loose, and it is easy for them to escape. When the spider bites the moth first, it succumbs to the poison and cannot escape while the spider is wrapping it up.

Some orb weavers carefully rebuild areas of the web damaged by prey, keeping their webs ever fresh and lovely. Others are less particular and merely repair loose strands so that the rest of the web retains the correct tension. Their webs can look pretty shabby after awhile. While many species build a new web every day, commonly at least the bridge line is used over and over again. The spiral of ecribellate spiders must be renewed every day, for it loses its stickiness by then. It may seem wasteful that the spider takes down its web each day. But by doing so, it may be removing a clue which enemies use to find it.

Six

The Hunters

Webs make very useful traps for entangling prey, but many spiders do perfectly well without them. Strong legs and sharp fangs are fine weapons for overpowering victims without the aid of silk. Hunting spiders are abundant in places where webs might not be so convenient—in windy areas where webs might be damaged, and in deserts, where there are few plants on which to hang webs. In our eastern forests, half the spiders are web-builders, while on the western deserts, only 20 to 30 percent rely on silk to capture their prey.

The variety of hunting spiders is very great. Some are so small and secretive that we rarely if ever come across them, while others, like wolf and jumping spiders, are familiar to most people. Some of the least well known types are primitive sorts which have never gotten around to web building as a way of life. They are thought to be closer to the ancestors of all spiders, which lurked in prehistoric forests, coming out mostly at night to grope along the ground for their prey. Among these spiders are some which use silk to some extent to aid their hunting. Ariadna, a common American spider, lives in a silken tube built in a rock wall or other protected spot. The tube has a silk collar around its entrance. From this collar, two dozen or so heavy, radial lines of silk stretch out and are anchored a short distance

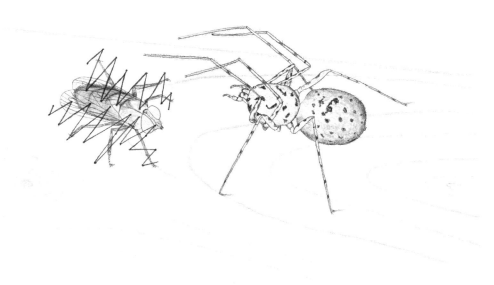

The spitting spider Scytodes pins down its prey with sticky zigzags of glue. Glands in the fat cephalothorax produce this effective trapping material. DRAWING BY THE AUTHOR.

away. The lines project above the surface a bit, for they are supported by tiny silken props near the collar and a bit beyond. Ariadna sits in the entrance to the tube with six legs reaching outward. When an insect trips on one of the radial lines, out rushes the spider in a flash and grabs it, rushing instantly back into the safety of the nest with the victim. The silken tube is narrow; and large, potentially dangerous insects such as wasps are grabbed in the middle and helplessly bent in two as they are dragged into the nest, their stingers pointing safely away from the little hunter.

The Spitting Spider

One more primitive spider utilizes a technique every bit as effective as a silken web for entangling its prey. The spitting spider Scytodes looks little like a hunter. It is slow-moving with weak, skinny legs hardly fit for overwhelming prey. Its fat cephalothorax, which gives it an awkward look, harbors a secret weapon. Its poison glands are enormously enlarged to produce not only venom but also a unique, sticky glue which it spits at its victims. When Scytodes touches a potential meal with one of its front legs, its response is immediate. In a fraction of a second, its vibrating body spits out gummy glue in a zig-zag pattern, pinning the victim instantly to the ground. Each fang squirts out 10 to 20 threads which meet in the middle of the victim, holding it firmly down. The spider can then leisurely attack, biting the prey repeatedly on the legs until it is dead. Then Scytodes cuts free its meal, dragging it off to a sheltered place to feed.

The gum can also be used as a defense against enemies. If attacked by a predator such as a scorpion, Scytodes shoots out its glue and the attacker lets it go, retreating some distance before cleaning off the sticky stuff.

Hunters and Wanderers

While spiders in many families live without webs, there are two main lines of more advanced hunting spiders. Web-builders use the third unpaired claws on their tarsi to swing their way through aerial snares; these hooks have little use for a spider running along the ground and among the plants. Spiders in one line of hunters, however, still have this claw, although it is not used as a hook. These are the wolf, fisher, and lynx spiders, many of which live in the United States. Lynx spiders live mostly on plants, leaping gracefully from leaf to leaf and hunting largely during the daytime. Lynx spiders often sport bright green bodies which camouflage them among the plants where they live. Western species

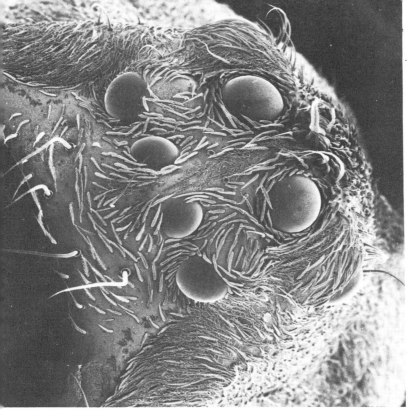

The fisher spider, Pisaura, also called the nursery web spider, is a powerful hunter with eight large eyes. As this portrait shows, each eye points in a different direction. Notice the two eyes just visible on the sides of the head near the top. DR. R. F. FOELIX

which live in woody shrubs such as buckwheat or sagebrush are brown or grayish in color.

Fisher spiders are not especially familiar to most of us, for they live along the shores of streams and lakes. The name fisher is entirely suitable for these large and handsome creatures, for they lurk along the shoreline, waiting for insects which become trapped in the water's surface film. Upon spying a struggling insect, the fisher spider races out across the surface and grabs it. The fisher spider can also dive beneath the surface and remain there as long as 45 minutes, silver bubbles of air clinging to its body and providing it with oxygen during the dive. Fisher spiders feed not only on waterlogged insects but also upon shoreline and aquatic insects and small fish. Whatever its prey, the fisher must emerge from the water to feed, for its digestive juices would merely be washed away in the water.

Wolf Spiders

Wolf spiders (Lycosidae) are among the most varied and common spiders. They have adapted to life just about everywhere, from the seashore to the desert, from the far north to the torrid south. Wolf spiders vary greatly in size as well, ranging from ⅔ centimeter (¼ inch) to about 4 centimeters (more than 1½ inches). Many wolf spiders cling to life in silken retreats, some even with trap doors, and a few have gone over to spinning sheet-like webs. But plenty of them have given up the homebody life completely and wander about over the ground, using their superior eyesight and strong jaws to overwhelm their prey.

Despite their variety of life styles, however, wolf spiders are easily recognizable. The wolf spider cephalothorax is elongated and is about the same size as the abdomen. Striped browns and grays are common colors, and a coat of fine hairs reinforces the common name of these fierce looking hunters. Wolf spiders, unlike some of their relatives, have what could be called a real face, with the front of the cephalothorax rounded on top and flattened in front. The position and size of the eyes is especially striking. Just above the large, toothed chelicerae is a row of four small eyes. Above them lies a pair of two much larger eyes, also facing forward. A bit higher, pointing towards the sides, are two more large eyes which peer sideways. With this

Wolf spiders are expert hunters that use their large eyes to spot prey and their strong chelicerae to subdue it. This Lycosa carolinensis *has captured a corn earworm moth.* PHILIP S. CALLAHAN

battery of eyes, the wolf spider can see in just about any direction.

The wolf spider is a powerful hunter. It can course rapidly and steadily along in pursuit of prey and then pounce, delivering the fatal bite with its sharp fangs, while holding on with its powerful front legs. While many spiders inject their digestive enzymes and suck their victims dry, wolf spiders crush their food with the sharp teeth on their sturdy chelicerae.

These strong chelicerae are also useful in digging burrows. Many wolf spiders, even though they are running hunters, dig complex burrows to which they return for rest and protection. The sand or dirt is dug loose with the chelicerae. Then the bits of soil are bundled up into little pellets bound together with silk. The spider carries the pellets out of the burrow and drops them away from the entrance. The tunnel is lined with silk and has a widened "living room" near the middle where the spider can rest comfortably and can turn around.

Some wolf spiders are especially well adapted to life along the seashore. One British species makes its home among the coarse grasses of the salt flats. When the tide comes in, this wolf spider heads for the tops of the plants, as if attempting to escape from the rising waters. But then it does a peculiar thing. Instead of clinging to the plant top, the spider turns around and walks deliberately down to the base of the stem, under the water's surface. An air bubble clings to the animal's hairy body and provides it with enough oxygen to last through high tide. Actually, the bubble can last as long as 10 hours, more than enough to survive the tide. By clinging to the plants, this little diver is protected from bobbing to the surface and being washed away.

The fierce look of the wolf spider has sometimes gotten it into trouble. The Italian wolf spider, *Lycosa tarentula*, got its name from its home area around the city of Taranto in southern Italy. In the late 14th century, word started getting around that this innocent spider gave a terrible bite causing pain, swelling, nausea, delirium, and other unpleasant and alarming symptoms. The only cure, it was thought, was wild and vigorous dancing, accompanied by special music for the occasion. For the next three hundred years or more, waves of this supposed disease swept through southern Europe and people by the dozens fell victim to it. Even as late as 1866, a book written about tarantism claimed that the disease was real and caused by the innocent wolf spider, and that only dancing to music could cure it. Historians and scientists puzzling over this prolonged wave of hysteria are not sure of its cause. Some believe that the dancers were not sick at all, but merely used the spider as an excuse to indulge in old pagan dancing and rituals which had been supressed by Christianity. Others think that the victims were really bitten by a spider—not the wolf spider but rather the Italian version of the black widow. The symptoms of tarantism do resemble those of a black widow bite. But just how the whole phenomenon came to be blamed on a harmless wolf spider will always be a puzzle. Today, the only reminder of this strange thread of history is the very vigorous Italian folk dance called the tarantella.

Jumping Spiders

Jumping spiders (Salticidae) are champion active hunters. Their quick darts and long leaps quickly distinguish them from the more smoothly running wolf spiders, as do their chunky bodies and shorter legs. Jumping spiders and their somewhat distant relatives, the crab spiders, represent the other line of active spiders which have shunned the web-bound way of life. They completely lack the third claw on their tarsi but have instead tufts of tiny, sticky claws which enable them to climb surfaces as slick and steep as windows and bathtubs.

Jumping spiders in general are small, rarely reaching over 1¼ centimeters (½ inch) in length. These most colorful spiders are not often appreciated for their beauty because of their size, but some tropical species have an even greater brilliance and glow to their blues and greens than the famous morpho butterflies and birds of paradise. American jumpers, too, are often brightly colored, especially the males, which often possess special tufts and clumps of bright hairs shown off during courtship.

Salticids have even better vision that wolf spiders. Their eyes are arranged differently, too. The largest pair is on the front of the face, with two smaller eyes to the sides and somewhat above. Nearer the top of the head is the third eye pair, often so small as to pass unnoticed. The final pair of eyes is located near the top of the head and points upward and to the sides. The six smaller eyes have a simple structure similar to that of other spider eyes. But the principal eyes, which give the jumping spider's face its look of personality, can be moved and are very complex in structure. Each eye has six muscles to move it this way and that; actually, it is only the sensitive part of the eye (the retina) which moves. With these eyes, the jumping spider can perceive sharp images from 25 to 30 centimeters (10 to 12 inches) away.

Their keen eyesight allows salticids to gauge distances very accurately and jump many times their own body length to precise landings. Just in case, however, the jumper anchors down its dragline before taking off. Then, if it misses its target, the spider merely ends up hanging in the air, safely suspended.

Crab Spiders

While jumping spiders are active, go-getting hunters, crab spiders are mainly sit-and-wait ambushers. Some of these chunky spiders with flattened bodies hide under bark or in crevices, while others sit on flowers awaiting the arrival of bees and wasps, which they promptly attack. The front two pairs of legs in these ambushers are sometimes quite long and are held out to the sides, twisted so that the claws face forward rather than downward. When a bee intent on

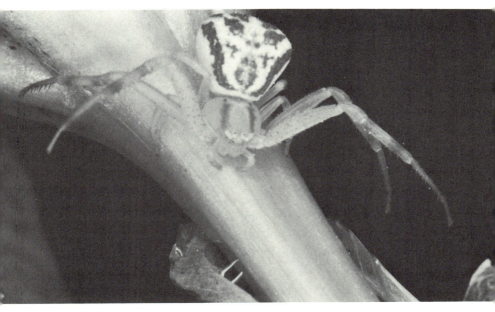

Crab spiders lie in wait and ambush their prey, using their long, strong legs to capture it. DR. HERBERT W. LEVI

collecting pollen or nectar lands, the crab spider instantly grabs it with these pincer-like legs and bites, injecting an especially potent venom. Then it settles down to feed.

Flower-hiding crab spiders are often white or yellow, which camouflages them against their floral background. Some can change colors, depending on the color of the background they have chosen. Adult females of one kind are white, but change to yellow in one to twenty days if placed on a yellow flower. If then moved to a white flower, the spider changes back to white in only five or six days. This trick is accomplished by yellow pigment which moves from the wall of the intestine to the skin to make the spider yellow. When the spider is white, the yellow pigment in the intestinal wall is hidden by white reflecting crystals under the transparent skin.

Using a Unique Technique

Despite its close relationship with orb web builders, the bolas spider has given up the web completely. This fat, lazy spider, camouflaged to resemble a bud, a nut, or a bit of debris, remains quiet during daylight hours. When night falls, she goes to work. She lays down a strong, loose line which is fastened down at both ends. She hangs from this line and produces her remarkable weapon, a blob of sticky silk hanging from a strong thread. Holding the end of the thread, the bolas spider waits for the approach of prey. When an insect comes within range of her sticky ball, the bolas spider flings it towards the victim, which becomes trapped in the gooey glob. The spider then bites the struggling prey, quieting it quickly, and wraps it before sucking it out.

At first it seems hard to understand how a spider could be assured of capturing an adequate food supply by this method. But biologists investigating the bolas spider believe that it uses an additional trick. They found that her prey consists almost exclusively of certain night-flying moths, and only males at that. The females of these moths release an attractive perfume into the air to attract mates. The bolas spider probably produces these same chemicals, or similar ones, which attract male moths to their death. Only female bolas spiders feed in this fashion, for the males hatch out of the egg sac as miniature, completely mature adults, ready for mating.

The Water Spider

While some people use the term "water spider" for the fisher spiders, this term should be reserved for the one spider which truly dwells underwater—Argyroneta. Although many spiders can climb under water while hanging onto plants and can remain there for rather long periods of time, only Argyroneta actually builds a web, feeds, and lays her eggs under water. Nothing about the appearance of this spider marks it as especially different. It is about 1¼ centimeters (½ inch) long and plain dark brown. But when it dips below the surface, the thin film of air covering its body turns Argyroneta into a bubble of shining silver. Attached to underwater plants, Argyroneta builds a dense sheet of silk. Then it goes to the surface and traps an air bubble beneath its body, holding the bubble in place with brushes of hairs on its hind legs. It returns to the silken sheet and releases the bubble underneath. The silk balloons upward and traps the bubble. The spider repeats this activity several times, making a good-sized bubble from all the small ones. Then it spins additional threads of silk around this diving bell, securing it into the roof of silk.

All its vital life activities take place within the water spider's airy home. There it feeds, mates, raises its family, and molts. When mating time comes, the male spider places his diving bell next to that of his mate and builds a silk tunnel to join their nests.

The spider hunts mainly at night, bringing the aquatic insects it captures back to the diving bell to be eaten. When winter comes, the spider builds a sturdy home inside an empty snail shell or other shelter on the bottom. There it spends the cold months in a sort of suspended animation, its body functions running at such a slow rate that it need not renew its oxygen supply again before spring.

Seven

Poisonous Spiders

In many parts of the world, people are so afraid of spiders that all are considered dangerous. While it is true that poisonous spiders are a more serious public health problem in some countries than poisonous snakes, the vast majority of spiders are completely harmless to humans. The bites of some spiders are painful and may cause some swelling and pain. But only a very few spiders have venom strong enough to kill a person, and even those spiders are much more likely to make a person very ill rather than actually kill him or her. Because of their small size, children are more likely to be killed by a spider bite than are adults.

Pinning down just how dangerous a particular species of spider is can be difficult. Many spiders, such as our tarantulas, are wrongly accused of being poisonous to people. One spider species may be quite dangerous, while a close relative is absolutely harmless. Some poisonous spiders, such as the black widow, are shy and rarely actually bite, while others may be irritable and bite with little provocation. Male spiders usually do not have enough venom to kill a person, while females may be especially aggressive while guarding an egg sac or spiderlings. The seriousness of a bite is also influenced by its location, the amount of venom injected, and the depth of the bite. Some persons bitten by black widows, for example, have suffered almost no symptoms at all, either because the bite was not deep or because the spider did not inject any venom.

Among the mygales, notoriously poisonous spiders are found in three families. Poisonous species live in Central and South America, Australia and New Zealand, and South Africa. Some of these have venom strong enough to kill people. One kind, called Trechona, lives in holes or along forest paths in the eastern parts of South America. If disturbed, Trechona rears up threateningly and bites readily. Atrax, which lives in Australia, is a small funnel-web building mygale. Two species can kill people. These brown spiders spend most of their lives in their webs. But when the mating season comes they may wander about and enter houses. If disturbed by people they can be quite aggressive, jumping as far as 10 centimeters (4 inches) onto a victim. In South Africa the 2 to 3 centimeter (about an inch)-long spider Harpactirella is much feared. While it inhabits a silk-lined nest under stones and logs, it also often enters houses. It can climb smooth surfaces such as walls, and is ready to attack the moment it is disturbed.

Any of these three spiders can kill people with its bite. While none bites without being provoked, what is provocation from the spider's point of view can be something as innocent as the movements of a child turning over in bed while asleep. Several other mygales have painful bites which may result in illness, but none are known for certain to have caused human death.

Poisonous "True" Spiders

Those true spiders known to be, or suspected of being, especially dangerous to people are scattered among a few spider families. Phoneutria is a spider which belongs to a small family (Ctenidae) of rather large hunters, often similar in appearance to wolf spiders. Phoneutria has the most potent of spider venoms, a paralyzing nerve poison. The spiders run about at night and may seek shelter in clothing or shoes when morning dawns. These spiders are especially aggressive and attack at the smallest excuse, perhaps biting the same victim viciously several times. Phoneutria is especially common in Brazil.

A particularly alarming type of venom is injected by some South American wolf spiders. Like Phoneutria, these hunters wander about at night and may seek refuge in shoes or clothing, biting the person as he gets dressed in the morning. The bite is very painful and causes the cells around it to die. If the bite is in a place where blood circulation is good, it rarely develops into a serious wound. But if it occurs in a location where the skin is thick and little blood circulation occurs, such as the sole of the foot, the area of dying tissue can become very large, and the wound may not heal without medical treatment.

Some American web-building spiders (Loxosceles) have a similar sort of venom. One of these, called the brown recluse, is found in the southern United States and may be increasing its range. The corner spider of Chile is an especially poisonous Loxosceles. Wounds from its bites may reach over 15 centimeters (6 inches) in diameter, and healing can take as long as 100 days. Like so many other spiders, the corner spider can live quite comfortably inside buildings and may hide inside boxes and clothing. In recent years, these spiders have been found living in some buildings in the United States.

Brown recluse venom is similar to that of the corner spider but apparently not so potent. The brown recluse can be distinguished from other brown house spiders by the violin-shaped marking on the top of the cephalothorax. This marking leads to its other common names—violin spider or fiddleback spider. The brown recluse also has only six eyes,

The poisonous brown recluse has a distinctive violin-shaped marking on its back which is lacking in other brown spiders that live in houses. This unique marking leads to its other common names—fiddle-back spider and violin spider. USDA

arranged on its face in three separate groups of two. While it resides out-of-doors in some midwestern and southern states, it lives in houses in more northerly areas. Now and then one shows up in such states as California, New Jersey, Arizona, Minnesota, or Florida, all far outside its natural range. Other species of Loxosceles are found in the western deserts, and their bite may also be severe, but little is known about them.

Effects of a brown recluse bite appear slowly. Several

hours after the bite, a blister appears. Bit by bit, the area around the blister turns purple and then black as the cells die off. The eventual wound is usually 2½ to 5 centimeters (1 to 2 inches) in diameter and can be healed with proper medical treatment. But a few unfortunate people are especially sensitive to brown recluse venom and suffer serious or even fatal symptoms.

Widow Spiders

By far the most widespread and familiar poisonous spiders are the widow spiders. Various species of these dangerous creatures are found almost worldwide. Widow spiders have a fat abdomen and a small cephalothorax. Most are glossy black with red or white markings on the abdomen. While not very large—usually no more than a centimeter (¹⁄₁₀ inch) long—the female widow spider has a potent venom indeed; the male is harmless. While the brown recluse and its cousins produce a serious local wound, a widow spider bite is so inconspicuous that it is sometimes hard to find. The effects of the poison are on the nervous systems and muscles. Within a few minutes of the bite, the victim begins to feel painful swelling in the lymph glands nearest the bite. Soon the thigh muscles and back muscles begin to hurt intensely, and the abdominal muscles become hard. The pain is excruciating. Breathing may become difficult, and the victim may sweat heavily. Other symptoms, such as nausea, vomiting, restlessness, and puffiness may also occur. Altogether, it is a very nasty and painful experience. But few people actually die from widow spider bites. Most adults suffer from these intense symptoms for from one to four days and may require some weeks for a complete recovery. Children who are bitten are much more likely to die from the bite. Fortunately, an antiserum is now available to treat black widow victims. Over the entire United States, fewer than 10 people die each year from widow spider bites.

There are actually five different species of widow spiders in the United States. The brown widow is basically a tropical species, common in eastern South America but found in the U.S. only in southern Florida. The red widow also lives in Florida. It has bright orange or reddish legs, and its abdomen is spotted with bright red or yellow marks. The red widow lives among palmetto plants, building its web between the fronds. Its retreat is made by rolling up a frond into a cone and lining it with silk. There are apparently no records of bites by the red widow, so we do not know if this spider is poisonous like its relatives.

Black Widows

Three kinds of black widows live in the United States. Females of all three are black with red markings on the underside of the abdomen. Most have an obvious red hourglass, but sometimes there are two separate red marks instead, and other red marks may also be present. Despite the medical importance of these animals, only recently have biologists agreed on the number and ranges of the different species. Although it has been known since the 1930's that black widows live in our northern areas, even recent books often proclaim that they are common, or occur at all, only in the South. Some books say that only the southern widows are dangerous. But in fact, more black widow bites occur in California than in any other state. These spiders live in *all* 48 lower states and even into some areas of Canada. They may be extremely common, even in the North, and northern and western widows may cause severe illness. Recently I learned of a man bitten in the state of Washington by a black widow which fell into his boot as he was riding horse-

Male and female black widow spiders look quite different. The female, on the left, is black, with red markings on the underside of her abdomen. The male, right, is much smaller than the female and has light markings on his body. Notice the enlarged palps of the male. USDA

back. His leg swelled up greatly and he was so sick the doctors thought he would die. After weeks of illness, he finally recovered. But even months after the incident, he still had recurrent pain in the bitten leg.

Where I live in Montana, black widows are very common.

In the fall of 1978, we captured about a dozen of them in our garage, basement, and house, and one in a bedroom. All these spiders were adult females, apparently looking for a sheltered place to spend the winter. This summer we had black widows in our window wells, and we just removed one from her rather large web in our basement. It is very difficult to get rid of these spiders, for they seem to be quite resistant to insecticides. And, at the slightest disturbance, the spiders beat a hasty retreat into cracks where they cannot be reached.

This shyness is fortunate, given the commonness of black widows around buildings. Crevices and crannies are the natural habitat of this beautiful creature, and houses and barns provide plenty of them. Most black widow bites in earlier days occurred in outhouses. Since they are generally dark places, inhabited by lots of flies, outhouses make perfect black widow homes. Because of this unfortunate coincidence, most black widow bites were made on the private parts of the body. With the steady increase in indoor plumbing facilities, fewer bites have occurred.

Scientists have learned some interesting facts about black widow venom. It contains four different poisonous components. Three of these are effective on insect prey, while the other works on warm-blooded animals, presumably enemies of the spiders. When the spider bites an insect, one of the poisons has a rapid paralyzing effect. Then the other two poisons go to work, slowly killing the victim by damaging its nervous system beyond repair.

The widow poison dangerous to warm-blooded animals, including humans, acts by interfering with the transmission of nervous impulses, especially those to the muscles—hence, the severe muscle pain associated with the bite.

Eight
From One Generation
to the Next

Reproduction in many animals is a relatively simple affair. The males and females of many sea creatures merely release their sperms and eggs into the water. The sperms fertilize the eggs, and the new generation begins. Land animals have more complicated reproduction, for sperms cannot live in the drying air. For this reason, the eggs of land animals are fertilized inside the body of the female, and the animals must mate for this to occur. The transfer of sperms into the female's body is often preceded by courtship behavior which allows the male and female to recognize one another and gets them both ready to mate at the same time. Among land animals, spiders have some of the most puzzling and fascinating adaptations to mating. The spider way of doing things in some cases seems needlessly complex to human understanding, but the methods have served spiders well.

The males of many spiders are smaller than the females. Females of some large orb web spiders weigh 100 or even 1,000 times as much as the males. Even when the two sexes are similar in size, as in tarantulas, the males tend to be more slightly built and have longer legs than the females. This is probably because the female spiders are the stay-at-homes, while the males must wander about in search of mates. Lighter bodies and longer legs would make traveling easier.

As long as spiders are immature, males and females tend to look very much alike. Males often reach adulthood at an earlier age and with fewer molts than do females. The signs of sexual maturity only appear with the final molt. Immature male tarantulas, for example, look much like females. But with the final molt, males develop hooks on their front legs which are absent in females. Adult males of some spiders, especially jumping spiders, are much more colorful than their mates. The pedipalps of adult males are also diffferent from those of females. They may have extra spines and hooks, and sometimes they are very much enlarged.

There is a good reason for the different structure of the male pedipalps, for they are used by the male to transfer sperm into the female's body. Most male land animals have a sperm transfer organ, such as a penis, which connects directly with the testes (internal organs where sperms are produced), but not spiders. The male spider, before mating, must transfer sperms from the genital opening (which connects the testes to the outside) into special hollow chambers in the palps, which are the tips of the pedipalps. This process is called "sperm induction." The way this is done seems very peculiar to us, but to spiders it is normal.

As the first step in sperm induction, the male spider spins a small web. Then he rubs his genital opening over the web, releasing a drop of liquid containing sperms. Finally, he dips the tips of his pedipalps into the sperm droplet and sucks up the liquid. Often the male spider reaches through the web from the other side to collect the sperm. Sperm induction may take several hours, as in some tarantulas, or it may take no more than a few minutes, as in some small wolf spiders.

Once the male has filled his palps with sperm, he goes off

looking for a mate. If he belongs to a web-spinning species, he abandons his web and most likely will not feed again. Male tarantulas may wander in quite large numbers across roads during the mating season, and many die under the wheels of cars. The male locates the female by one of several methods. Short-sighted spiders which do not build webs, such as tarantulas, may recognize her by touch. Web-builders can recognize the silk of a female's web when they come across it, while a male wolf spider will court another spider, even a male, on sight.

The chemical sense is often used to find a mate. Many biologists believe that special hairs located on the tarsi of the legs can sense chemicals by touch. This sense is not quite like any human one. It is closer to taste than to smell, since the hairs must actually come into contact with the chemical to perceive it. Females of some spider species may release attractive chemicals into the air, and the silk laid down by others, including the black widow and some wolf spiders, contains a chemical which excites the male.

The Dangers of Mating

Because the female spider is an eager predator, the male must be careful when he approaches her for mating. If she does not recognize him as a mate, he may end up as a meal instead. Most spider males first court the female from a safe distance, being sure to get their point across before coming within reach. Males of some species are especially cautious, waiting to approach until the female is busily feeding. The male of one European wolf spider plays it especially safe; he captures a fly, wraps it up, and gives it to the female. While she is busy feeding, the male mates with her, then joins her at the feast.

There are other ways male spiders protect themselves

from their dangerous mates. The male Tetragnatha has special tooth-like, sturdy spines on his chelicerae. As the two spiders approach one another to mate, their chelicerae are wide open. The male hooks the special teeth onto the female's fangs, wedging them harmlessly open while mating takes place. Some males in another family (Linyphiidae) have very peculiarly shaped heads. W. S. Bristowe, a great British arachnologist, observed the mating of one species of these spiders and was amazed to see the female lunge at the male with her fangs bared. The male, instead of beating a hasty retreat, merely drew in his legs and waited passively. The female grabbed the male's head with her fangs, which came harmlessly to rest in the grooves along the sides of his head while he mated with her. The entire process was repeated several times.

Tarantula Mating

The male tarantula is big enough to be a match for his mate, and tarantula mating involves only a few preliminaries. When the male touches the female, he begins to tap her body with his first four legs. If the female is not ready to mate, she may run off. If she stays, she raises her own front legs in a pose suggestive of self-defense. As the male drums on her body, she rises up higher and higher, finally opening her fangs as if to bite. The male then grabs her chelicerae with the special hooks on his front legs, jamming them open. Now there is no way the female can hurt him. While she is reared up in this fashion, the male slips the tips of his palps into the special slits on the underside of her abdomen which lead to sperm storage chambers. There he deposits his sperm. This method, with some modification, is used by all spiders. The whole tarantula mating process usually takes only a few minutes, and the male leaves without the female trying to attack him.

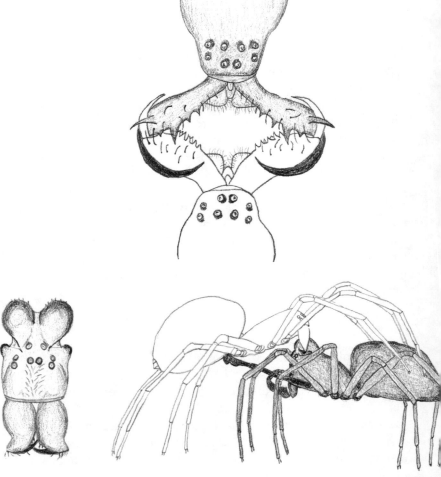

Some male spiders have ways of protecting themselves from the strong chelicerae of their mates. At the top, the male Tetragnatha *(with the dark head) has jammed open the chelicerae of his mate with the spines on his chelicerae. On the left, below, is the face of the male* Hypomma bituberculatum, *showing the bumps on top and the grooves into which the female's fangs fit while they are mating. At right, the female (light spider) grabs onto the male's head while he mates with her, using one palp at a time.*
DRAWING BY THE AUTHOR.

Some other spiders have simple courtship and mating. Crab spider males climb right up on females when they find them, and the females do not seem to object. Some crab spider males spin silk lines, attaching the abdomen and legs of the female to the leaves or ground. This thin webbing has been given the fanciful name "bridal veil."

Strumming and Drumming

Males of web-building spiders must approach the female on her web without being mistaken for prey. Many biologists believe web-building males are often small because tiny males would seem less like food than big ones. The males of some tropical orb web builders are even smaller than the smallest prey the females will eat. Male web builders often get around the problem of getting to the female without being eaten by sending vibration signals to her through the web which differ from the signals coming from struggling prey.

Male black widows are quite a bit smaller than the females and are differently shaped. Shortly after molting into the mature adult, the black widow male fills his palps with sperm and heads off in search of a mate. When he encounters silk spun by a female he becomes excited, his body quivering. Even if the silk is from a young female the male responds, for he may hang around her web until she molts into a mature female he can mate with.

As soon as he enters the web, the male begins to send his special signals. He taps the threads and plucks them with his front tarsi. As he moves along, he also uses his palps to tap the lines rhythmically. His body vibrates and jerks now and then as he explores the web. Here and there he rests. The female may not appreciate these attentions and may charge at the male, sending him into a quick retreat, often by way of his safety dragline off the web. If she tolerates him, the male cuts threads of the web near the female, making it hard for her to escape. A receptive female reacts to courtship by jerking and twitching, and soon the male approaches her directly, stroking her legs and abdomen, then climbing onto her body. He sometimes throws silk over her as he courts. Then they mate.

The whole courtship may last as little as 10 minutes or as long as 2 hours. After it is over, the male takes his time leaving. He does not seem to be aware of his mate's reputation as a do-it-yourself widow maker! Only occasionally does the female actually live up to her name and kill her mate.

Dancing and Tapping

Orb weavers lacking a cribellum (Araneidae) have an interesting variety of courtship patterns. Males of some species must brave the female's web to court her in the hub. The male must carefully cross the prey-capture area of the web, vibrating as he comes so that she will not mistake him for a meal. If he reaches the hub successfully, he then begins courting by stroking and tapping her. The male is so small in some species that he must crawl onto the underside of her abdomen, letting out his dragline for security, as she sits upside down in the hub of the web. Some orb web males lay down silk on the female's body during courtship, too.

In some species of Argiope, courtship begins in the same way, with the male courting the female at the hub. But then comes an interesting twist. The male cuts out several threads of the web near the hub and lays down his own strand, called the "mating thread," across the gap. He climbs onto the mating thread and puts on a great show of leg rubbing, bouncing, jerking, and line slapping. After awhile, the female climbs out onto the thread to join him. She hangs upside down by her back two pairs of legs while they mate.

In the most common courtship of North America orb weavers, the male spider need not enter the female's web at all. He attaches his mating thread to the edge of her web and does all his dancing and drumming there. When she is ready to mate, she walks out onto the mating thread and hangs head downward. Often she will rush threateningly out at him at first, but he merely cuts the line and swings free. Sometimes several males will attach their threads to the web of one female and compete for her attentions. With this sort of courtship, the male has little to fear from his potential mate.

Prancing and Waving

While web spiders count on their sensitivity to vibrations in courtship, wolf and jumping spiders depend on their superior eyesight, although some of their drumming may convey messages through the ground. Males of these spiders often are very brightly colored and have special decorations accented in the mating dance—plumes on their heads, black or white hairs on their palps, and so forth. The palps and front legs, which are often waved in characteristic ways, usually have bands of color or striking hairs. Male wolf spiders are eager to court anything resembling a female, including other males. But while a male wolf spider cannot recognize another male on sight, he can recognize the courtship dance and responds to it with a threat display. The female, on the other hand, responds to the male with her own courtship movements, waving her forelegs and moving closer to the male. Many wolf spiders include sounds

Male wolf spiders, such as this Lycosa, *perform complex court-ship displays. Each species has its own routine involving waving of the front legs and/or pedipalps and movements of the body.*
PHILIP S. CALLAHAN

or vibrations of the ground in their courtship. These help the female orient towards the male.

The variety of male dances and displays in wolf and jumping spiders is quite amazing, with each species using a unique combination of leg waving, body quivering, dancing about, and body posturing to convey its vital message. For example, the male of one American wolf spider recognizes the dragline silk of a potential mate and follows it to find her. Contact with her silk brings on his mating dance, as does touching her body. Even the dead, crushed, freeze-dried body of a female excites the male, so some stimulating chemical must be present in the female cuticle or body hairs.

The courting male drums his palps rapidly on the ground. Then he stretches his front legs forward and shakes his body as he lowers his legs. A close relative has quite a different display. The male raises and lowers his front legs in turn while wiggling his palps one after the other. Another relative hardly uses his front legs at all but wigwags his pedipalps wildly while standing high on tiptoes. These strong differences in displays of closely related spiders make it easy for the females to identify males of their own kind.

Making the Egg Sac

Once mating has occurred, the female is ready to lay her eggs. She may not do so right away, for she can store the sperms from the male for quite awhile. Some female spiders produce several egg sacs from one mating before the year is out, while others make only one. Each species makes a characteristic sort of egg sac. Some are as round as balls, while others are flattened and lens-shaped. The lynx spiders make strange, spiny-looking egg sacs.

When she is ready to lay her eggs, the female spider spins out a sheet of silk onto which she deposits the eggs. They may be glued together in a mass or may be more loosely bound. Fine, fluffy silk may be spun around the eggs before the sac is completed. The female spins and molds the egg sac carefully until the protected, secure package is finished. Most spiders use a special set of silk glands for making their precious egg sacs.

The number of eggs laid in one sac varies greatly. Some large spiders may place more than 2,000 eggs in one sac, while very tiny spiders may lay only one or two eggs at a time. The usual number of eggs for most spiders is around 100. These may all be in one sac or may be spread out into several, depending on the species.

Nine
Spiders Living Together

After carefully knitting together the protective egg sac, many spiders place it in a hidden place and forget about it, their most important work in life finished. But others keep the sac close at hand and watch over it, while a few actually take care of the young spiders after they hatch. Even when the mother abandons the egg sac, the young spiders of many kinds stay together for the first few days of their lives. These sorts of associations are the first hints of social behavior, indications that the ferociously carnivorous spiders, known at times to feed on others of their own kind, do have the ability to tolerate and even cooperate with one another. This tendency has led to communal living in a few rather different sorts of spiders. In recent years, scientists studying these species have come up with some interesting facts about them.

Mothers and Babies

Many spider mothers care for their egg sacs. The black widow and others watch out for their egg sacs, moving them from their retreats out into the web and back inside again when they retire. The female cellar spider Pholcus carries her sac about in her chelicerae until the young are ready to hatch. She then hangs it in her web and guards the young as they emerge.

Sometimes related spiders show varying degrees of maternal care. The European comb-footed spider *Theridion saxatile*, which is such a block-and-tackle expert, keeps her egg sac in the nest she so carefully builds in the center of her web. The web is built in the protected cover of overhanging banks which face south, so the nest will sometimes heat up to dangerously high temperatures. Excessive heat can kill the spider embryos, so when it gets warmer than 30°C (86°F), the spider removes her egg sac from the nest and hangs it in the cooler web. When the heat dies down, she returns the sac to the nest.

After the young spiders hatch out, they stay in the web for about a month, feeding with their mother on prey she captures. When they are very tiny, the spiderlings stay in the nest while the mother kills the prey, but when they get older they help out, biting the victim and throwing threads of silk over it.

A close relative (*Theridion sisyphium*) actually feeds the young after they hatch. She hangs downward in the web, a drop of nutritious liquid hanging from her mouth. The spiderlings crowd around, jostling one another to get to the food. This mouth feeding continues for several days; then the young share in their mother's meals. Instead of biting the prey only once or twice, as she would otherwise do, the mother bites the prey all over, making many holes from which her spiderlings can feed.

Portable Families

Many wandering spiders care for their egg sacs until hatching. Jumping spiders, lynx spiders, and others stand

*Wolf spiders are very protective mothers. The female carries
her egg sac wherever she goes, above, and opens it when it is
time for the spiderlings to emerge, below. The baby spiders
then climb onto her body and go wherever she does, right, hanging on tightly for several days before setting out on their own.*
DR. R. F. FOELIX

guard over them until they hatch, while wolf and fisher spiders carry them about wherever they go. The female fisher spider hangs tightly onto her egg sac. Her fangs pierce its sides while her pedipalps grasp it firmly around the sides in front. Silk from her spinnerets anchors it securely beneath her body. The egg sac is often so large that the spider must totter around on tiptoe to keep from dragging it on the ground.

When the young are about to emerge, the fisher spider builds a small web underneath a leaf, pulling the edges down to form a secluded retreat, and hangs the egg sac there. When they hatch, the spiderlings live in this protected nursery, guarded by their mother until they venture off a week or so later.

The mother wolf spider has a better way of carrying her egg sac about. She attaches it to her spinnerets so that it can be dragged about behind her while she goes about her business. When the young spiders are ready to hatch, the mother bites open the egg sac; the spiderlings cannot cut through its tough covering by themselves. The babies then

climb up on their mother's back, covering her sometimes with more than one layer of tiny hitchhikers. Her abdomen is coated with special hairs which enable the babies to hang on. She goes about her normal business for the week or so that her young stay. They must cling for dear life while she rushes after prey and dashes away from enemies. Sometimes they hop off briefly for a drink of water and clamber back on hastily before she takes off again. The spiderlings do not feed during this time; apparently there is enough yolk in their bodies to nourish them until they molt and depart for lives of their own.

Spiderlings Together

When spiderlings actually leave the egg sac, they have already spent several days out of their eggs. They hatch from the eggs as partially developed embryos and lie helpless and unspiderlike, crammed together in the egg sac for some time before molting into miniature spiders and working their way out. Like wolf spider young, most newly emerged spiderlings have some yolk in their bodies and do not feed for the first few days. During this time, the young spiders may build a communal web and remain together on it for several days until they get hungry and become a danger to one another.

Once I approached such a nursery web in my back yard. At first I could not see the baby spiders, for they were spread out over the web. But as my footsteps approached, suddenly a tiny cloud of spider bodies appeared in the center of the web as all the spiderlings retreated into a ball. Perhaps by clustering together in this way the tiny spiders confuse and discourage small predators in search of bite-sized meals. Once the spiderlings use up their yolk, they disperse by ballooning as soon as the wind is right. From then on until their brief period of mating, they will live solitary lives.

Spider Societies

Despite the solitary ferocity of most spiders, quite a few species have evolved some form of mutual tolerance. Nine different families have species which live in groups. All of these families have mostly solitary species, so social association must have evolved separately in each case. Some of these spiders merely build their webs in a connected fashion, but others actually cooperate in building a shared web and even feed together on prey.

What forces would favor the development of cooperative behavior in spiders? The individual web is a very efficient trap, and the hostility which spiders show even for others of their kind would seem to make it difficult for them to tolerate one another. But cooperation does have its advantages. For one thing, a group of cooperating spiders can build a much bigger web than one single spider. This allows them to use large, open areas such as the spaces between trees and the gaps above wide streams as prey capture areas. A large web can also provide warning, through vibrations and/or behavior of the spiders, of predators. Spiderlings protected in a large colony would also have a better chance of survival than would lone, ballooning babies.

Communal Orb Weavers

The first requirement for cooperative behavior is merely tolerating members of the same species. Spiders could not exist in societies if they looked upon one another as prey.

The individual spiders also must be drawn towards one another; a spider must prefer to build its web next to that of another spider rather than separately. And, finally, there must be at least a minimum of cooperation among the spiders in establishing and maintaining the support lines of the communal web.

One Central American spider lives in communities with this sort of minimal social organization. From 5 to 70 spiders form a colony consisting of individual orbs constructed on common support lines. This results in a large web structure which spans streams, allowing the spiders to prey on the many small insects, especially flies, which navigate along the streams. Each spider lives on its own orb and ignores the other spiders in the colony. Their orbs rely on sticky spirals to capture prey, and each spider renews its spiral as often as three times in one day. Some locations in the web framework are better for prey capture than others. The spiders regularly switch positions, so they take turns living in the better and worse positions.

Even though each spider maintains and defends its own orb, very little fighting occurs between spiders, and cannibalism is almost nonexistent. The spiders do not cooperate in prey capture or in care of the young; each tends to its own life needs without help from the others. The only real cooperation is in keeping the support lines strong. Probably this spider shows as much social interaction as is possible in spiders which must maintain individual orbs requiring the daily care of sticky spiral renewal.

A progression in social association exists in the orb weaver Crytophora, which lives in New Guinea. Crytophora builds an orb without a sticky spiral. While this web is not as efficient at trapping flying insects as a sticky one, it need not be renewed so often and can survive heavy winds and rain much better. Most Crytophora species are completely solitary, but one kind is often found in loose aggregations of a few webs along hedges or fences. Another Crytophora species builds communal webs which span large spaces between trees. Night-flying moths use these spaces as flight paths and are a major source of food for the spiders. Solitary orb weavers cannot build webs large enough to span such distances. Like the Central American communal orb weaver, these Crytophora are able to capture prey which would otherwise be unavailable to them. But the individual nature of the orb web apparently has kept them from evolving more complex social interactions.

From Family to Society

Since mothers of many comb-footed spider species care for their young after hatching, it should not be surprising that some species have gone beyond early parental care to more permanent social behavior. *Anelosimus studiosus* lives in our southeastern states. Like some Theridion mothers, the female *A. studiosus* feeds her offspring by regurgitating food while they are very young. But instead of leaving after one or two molts, the young spiders stay on in the mother's web, helping her capture prey and cooperating in maintaining the sheet-and-snare web. The web becomes quite messy with prey remains and other debris, but by spinning new threads, the spiders keep it an effective snare.

Often the mother spider dies while her offspring are still quite young, but they still live together until the females mature. The mother, if she is still alive, or otherwise the first female to mature, forces the other females out of the web. They leave to found their own family colonies. The male spiders are smaller and weaker than the females and are always tolerated. However, they are not much good at

Females of Anelosimus studiosus *share their web and prey with their young. Here the spiderlings feed together on an insect while their mother, right, waits nearby. Males, such as the one on the left, are smaller than the females. They are always tolerated in the family web.* VINCENT BRACH

capturing prey and contribute little to the colony's well being.

The only real obstacle to more permanent colones than *A. studiosus* has is the antagonism between mature females. One Anelosimus species, *A. eximius*, has overcome that barrier and lives in huge colonies of hundreds or thousands of individuals of both sexes and all ages. Found in Brazil and Venezuela, the webs of *A. eximius* may completely cover shrubs or small trees. The webs may be about a meter (a yard) across and are made of light, transparent silk. The spiders capture food around the edges of the web and bring it to the center for feeding. The large webs, sometimes found 5 meters (15 feet) up in the trees, enable these small spiders to capture large flying insects which would otherwise be unavailable.

Tolerating One Another

Just what sort of mechanism keeps communal spiders such as *A. eximius* from attacking one another? Dr. J. Wesley Burgess has studied this problem in another social spider, *Mallos gregalis*, which lives in Mexico. *M. gregalis* is a small (2½ millimeter—$\frac{1}{10}$ inch) cribellate spider which lives in huge colonies with thousands of members. The communal web has a sticky surface sheet of cribellate silk and a lower region of complex chambers and tunnels. Holes in the surface lead to this inner region, where resting and egg-laying take place. The web of one colony may cover the trunk and branches of a good-size tree. The spiders specialize in capturing flies, which are several times as large as the spiders. By attacking the flies communally, the spiders are able to utilize prey much bigger than they could if they lived alone.

Mexicans call *M. gregalis* "el mosquero," the fly killer. During the rainy time of year, when flies are especially common, people living in the countryside around Guadalajara, where the spiders are common, sometimes bring web-covered branches into their homes as a sort of natural fly paper.

These spiders cooperate at least some in building and maintaining the web. One spider may finish a job begun by another, and one spider may cover the dry silk of a nestmate with cribellate threads. Males, females, and young spiders of all ages are tolerated, and the spiders never attack one another.

When a fly gets entangled in the web, it buzzes noisily as it tries to get free. The buzzing summons the spiders, who run out of the holes in the web and jerkily turn to face the buzzing fly. They hop quickily across the web towards the buzzing and bite the fly when they get to it. If the buzzing stops, the spiders freeze in place until it starts again, so it is evident that they are responding to the buzzing. The spiders do not paralyze the fly with their bites or wrap it, and the helpless insect only buzzes more loudly as it is bitten, until it dies. A subdued fly may be almost invisible under the swarm of spiders of all ages which feed peacefully together on its body.

In order to find out why the spiders attacked the flies and not one another, Dr. Burgess tested the web to see which vibrations it transmitted, and he studied the flies to see which vibrations they produced. He also tested the spiders to see how they responded to different vibration frequencies of the web. His results show that the web transmits certain vibrations made by buzzing flies and that the spiders respond to those same vibrations by coming out of their holes and heading for the source. The spiders do not respond to non-buzzing prey such as cockroaches or to insects, such as bees, which produce higher frequency vibrations.

Only buzzing flies in the web produce the signals which trigger the predatory response of these communal spiders. Since the spiders themselves never cause that sort of vibration in the web, they never bring out the predatory response in one another. They are protected from being mistakenly attacked and eaten by one another, since only a quite specific cue, the buzzing fly in the web, stimulates attack. The entire community benefits from this system, for the faster, stronger spiders reach the prey first and subdue it, and the younger and slower spiders, such as females ready to lay eggs, can join in afterward and share the prey.

Ten

Spiders and Other Animals

So far, we have looked at how spiders interact with their prey and with others of their own kind. Spiders interact with other animals in different ways, not only as predators. Spiders themselves serve as prey for a great variety of hunters, and spiders tolerate the nearness of certain other creatures without disturbing them. A surprising variety of spiders, too, look more like ants than like spiders, probably as a means of discouraging their own enemies.

Any animal which lives by catching small creatures could be an enemy of spiders. Frogs, toads, and lizards as well as birds and wasps may eat spiders. Although spider venom is usually harmless against vertebrate enemies, spiders are not completely defenseless. The ability to drop instantly and hang by a dragline has saved countless threatened spiders from sudden death. Some web-builders, such as the house spider Pholcus, will hang onto the web with all their legs and shake rapidly when alarmed. The whole web vibrates, creating a shapeless blur where once a spider sat. Spider legs and pedipalps break off readily between the first and second joints if pulled, and a spider can do perfectly well with fewer than eight legs. If immature spiders lose their limbs, they are regenerated when the animal molts. The new leg never reaches the size of a normal leg, and it takes at least three molts to grow one which is close to normal in size.

If a spider escapes an enemy with a wounded, bleeding leg or palp, it could prove fatal. Spider blood does not flow inside veins. It bathes the body tissues, so a spider can easily bleed to death. A spider with an injured leg grabs it with its other legs and mouth parts and pulls until it breaks off at the normal breaking point. This stops the bleeding.

When spiders are colored like their surroundings, they may be protected from predators as well as hidden from their intended prey. While crab spiders take days or weeks to change color to match their surroundings, a few spiders can change color rapidly. This sudden color change probably confuses their enemies. An orb builder from Virginia has white markings on its abdomen that disappear like magic when the spider drops from its web in alarm. While the markings disappear quickly, they return much more slowly. A different, unrelated spider can also change color rapidly. When undisturbed, this spider has white markings which are caused by crystals in its intestinal cells. If the spider is shaken up, the cells contract and the spider takes on the brown color of its body fluids.

The Worst Enemies

One sort of enemy which spiders have a hard time dealing with are wasps of various kinds. People tend to think of wasps as social creatures, such as the paper wasps which live in small colonies. But many different kinds of wasps are completely solitary, associating with one another only for mating. Often these solitary wasps hunt spiders. Mud dauber wasps paralyze spiders with their stings and store them in earthen cells made from mud. After filling up a cell with helpless, paralyzed spiders, the wasp lays an egg and closes the cell. The spiders stay alive, for the wasp

Many wasps are deadly spider enemies. This Episyron *is sipping at body fluids oozing from the sting wound of its paralyzed prey. The wasp will haul the spider to a hiding place safe from ants, dig a nest, and bury the spider after laying an egg on its helpless body.* FRANK E. KURCZEWSKI

venom affects body muscles but not the heart muscle. When the egg hatches, the wasp grub has a nice supply of fresh food waiting for it. Different kinds of mud daubers concentrate on different kinds of spiders. One wasp species takes mostly orb builders and crab spiders, while another likes orb builders and comb-footed spiders, including the black widow. Apparently its powerful poison does not protect the black widow from this enemy.

Many burrowing spiders are plagued by wasp enemies. One northern burrowing wolf spider is attacked by a very efficient wasp. During the springtime, the mature female spiders are caring for young spiders in their closed burrows. In late June and in July, the mothers must open up their doors to let out the spiderlings. Then the open burrows are attacked by the wasps. The wasp attempts to enter the spider nest, while the spider tries to push the wasp aside and get out. The two animals are about the same size, and about half the time the wasp succeeds in stinging the spider.

But where one wasp fails another may succeed, and eventually, by the end of July, 99 percent of the female spiders with open burrows have fallen victim to the stinging wasps. After paralyzing its prey, the wasp removes it from the nest and goes to work. She digs a side tunnel in the spider's burrow and drags the spider into it. Then she lays one egg on the helpless victim, fills up the tunnel and nest with dirt, and cleans up the area around the old entrance so that only a slight depression in the ground remains. When the wasp egg hatches, the fully grown adult spider provides just enough food for it to grow to maturity in the safety of the hidden burrow. The wolf spider species is able to survive the death of almost all mature females because the wasps attack after the spiders have reproduced, not before.

The Tarantula Hawk

One of nature's great dramas is the struggle between the tarantula and its most deadly enemy, the tarantula hawk. These metallic blue-black or greenish wasps, named Pepsis, have earned their name well, for they almost always win in life-and-death battles with tarantulas many times their own size. Pepsis hunts along the ground, looking for tarantulas to paralyze. Male spiders are easier to find, but their smaller size makes them less desirable, and their long legs sometimes enable them to hold their bodies far enough above the ground that the wasp cannot easily sting. So although Pepsis sometimes attacks male tarantulas, females are a preferred target. Once the wasp finds a female tarantula, the battle begins. She may need to coax the spider from her burrow, but that seems to be no problem for this eager hunter.

Once the wasp and spider face off, the battle begins. But despite the larger size of the spider, the result of the fight is rarely in doubt. The wasp boldly walks up to the spider. Then, in a flash, she slips underneath the tarantula's body and grabs onto a leg. The tarantula tries to fight her off, rolling wildly around on the ground or raising up as high as she can and trying to bite the wasp, but she rarely wins out. Meanwhile, the wasp pokes around with her stinger until she finds a weak place in the spider cuticle, a joint where she can insert her paralyzing stinger. It only takes a few seconds for the wasp venom to have its effect once the stinger has found its mark. The wasp holds in the sting, probably injecting a good dose of venom, for many seconds.

After the spider is paralyzed, the wasp buries it. Sometimes the wasp has already made its nest, but other times it must still hunt for a good place to dig, dragging its gigantic prey for many meters over the ground as it searches. Sometimes it is hours before the spider is deposited in its grave, one wasp egg attached to her abdomen. The wasp covers up its burrow and leaves the spider to its fate of being eaten alive slowly.

Spider-hunting wasps are not free of danger themselves, for still different wasps may take over their hard-won prey. Some of these wait until the spider hunter has left, and destroy its egg before laying their own in its place. Others merely add their egg to the paralyzed spider body, some hiding it in a fold of the cuticle. The larva of the second wasp then kills the egg or larva of the first wasp so that it has the spider to itself.

Hangers-On

The spider web, with its hanging packets of juicy insects, is a tempting target for several different creatures. Hummingbirds sometimes feed on insects trapped in the webs of the giant orb weaver Nephila, and they may raid the web for soft silk to build their nests. Some creatures have developed ways of sharing the spider's web without being ensnared or attacked. Several moth species live in spider webs while they are caterpillars, feeding on prey remains. In the Los Angeles area, bugs share the webs of one common sheet and funnel web weaver. The bugs feed on honeysuckle flowers as well as on small insects caught in the web, which the spiders ignore. The bugs can walk easily along either surface of the web sheet.

On the island of Trinidad, bugs live in Pholcus webs. These creatures move so slowly and quietly through the web that they do not arouse the predatory reactions of their hosts. The bugs attack insects entangled in the web, piercing the prey with their long, pointed mouths and rapidly sucking them dry. During periods of food scarcity, the bugs also glean what nutrients remain in prey already sucked on by the spiders.

Many kinds of small flies live around spider webs. One biologist observed flies which move about on the web, share the spider's prey, and, in return, clean the mouthparts of their hosts. In Panama, Nephila is pestered by tiny flies which actually rest on its back. The flies sit there, hardly moving, until the spider has attacked a victim in the web and injected its digestive enzymes. When the surface of the prey becomes wet with its liquefied contents, the flies leave the spider and cluster on the prey, quickly sucking up the nutritious fluid until their bodies are swollen almost to bursting.

In Michigan, scorpion flies steal food outright from spider webs. The fly may walk onto the web from anchoring plants or may fly in and land right on a trapped insect. If it gets entangled itself, the fly merely daubs the web with a special brown liquid which immediately dissolves the webbing. The scorpion fly usually feeds right there in the web and leaves only if threatened by the spider. Sometimes the fly stands its ground against the spider, daubing it with the brown fluid and smearing it about. While the spider tries to clean itself, the fly can escape. Even with its defenses, however, the fly lives a dangerous life, for many scorpion flies end up as spider meals.

Spiders Living Off Spiders

Many comb-footed spiders prefer living in the webs of other spiders to making their own. Sometimes they attach their own webs to the edges of other webs, and other times they merely inhabit another's web, adding just a few of their own strands. As many as 50 of these spiders, sometimes from three different species, may live on one large orb, feeding on small insects ignored by their host, stealing packaged prey before the host can get to it, or even joining the host as it sucks on its prey.

Dr. Fritz Vollrath studied the behavior of one klepto-parasite, as these thieves are called, in Panama. This small spider, named *Argyrodes elevatus*, makes its home around the edges of large orbs made by Nephila or another orb weaver. Nephila females may be more than seven times as long as their "guests." In addition to her orb, Nephila builds a tangled web around the edges of the orb, called a barrier web. Many orb weavers build barrier webs, which may help warn the spiders of enemies approaching. The kleptoparasite lives in the barrier web, attaching a few of its own threads to the hub and to several radii of the orb. Through these strands, Argyrodes keeps tabs on Nephila's activities. When the orb weaver actually wraps up captured prey, the parasite is alerted and moves into the hub, where Nephila always stores her prey packets. Then, when Nephila next rushes out to attack an entangled insect, Argyrodes moves in with searching front legs, feeling around for the precious packet. When its feet touch the prey, it goes to work. It attaches securing threads to the packet, attaching them to points outside the orb. Then it cuts the host threads holding the packet one by one, each time anchoring its own dragline to them first, then easing the cut lines out slowly so that no big vibrations result. After cutting the prey packet out of the web, Argyrodes carries it off along the securing threads, out of the orb. Argyrodes accomplishes its work in a remarkably short time, locating the prey in as little as a second and taking only another 4 to 10 seconds to cut it free and carry it off. The stolen prey may weigh 10 times as much as the thief and is often too big for it actually to consume. Sometimes, instead of moving right into the hub when Nephila wraps her prey, the kleptoparasite waits to enter the web until the host attacks a new victim. Since this gives it less time to find and steal the food, Argyrodes is less successful when it uses this technique.

When Nephila returns to the hub, she may sense the disappearance of her food. She searches and searches about the hub for the missing packet, plucking first this radius and then that, trying to find it. She may then climb out onto the barrier web and shake it violently, feeling for the vibrations of a swinging prey packet. Occasionally this strategy works and Nephila retrieves her stolen food. But usually, once the kleptoparasite has cut all threads leading to the prey, the food is lost to its rightful owner.

Spider-Killing Spiders

W. S. Bristowe has said that spiders are the worst enemies of spiders, for these cannibals will attack the eggs, young, and even adults of others of their own species. Many spiders fall prey to spiders of other species, too, as when hunting spiders blunder into webs or web-builders are caught by hunters outside their webs.

But the deadliest spiders from the spider point of view are hunters which specialize in feeding on other spiders. The pirate spiders (Mimetidae) rarely consume insects, for other spiders are their favorite food. Ero is a small but deadly pirate which often preys on comb-footed spiders. Ero slowly and quietly enters the web of its intended victim, cutting out threads of the web to clear the way for its deadly act. Then Ero tugs at the web lines as if it were an ensnared insect, and the web owner rushes over to attack its "prey." But Ero is waiting and reaches out with lightning speed to grab the leg of its victim with its long front legs. Spines on the legs hold firmly onto the victims leg while Ero quickly bites, almost immediately killing its victim. The strong venom acts so fast that the only sign, if any, given by the victim is a slight tremor before dying.

Spider or Ant?

Some spiders look so much like ants that they can fool even the experts at first glance. Other spiders look antlike enough that the first look is followed by a double take. Ant "copying," or mimicry, is found in eight different spider families, often in many species. Why should this be so?

One reason ants are such common and obvious animals is that they are not the tastiest of creatures. Most ants produce unpleasant substances, such as formic acid, which they use in defending themselves from enemies. These chemicals make them taste bad, too. Many ants, especially larger species, are also quite fierce and will fearlessly attack anything which threatens them. For these reasons, most animals not specialized as ant predators usually leave them alone.

Biologists have often argued about the advantages of

ant mimicry. Do spiders look like ants to avoid their own predators, or do they resemble them so they can get closer and prey on them? The more we learn about these interesting spiders, the more it seems that resemblance to ants is an effective protection from predators, not a ploy to fool prey. While a few ant mimics actually live in ant nests and feed on ant pupas, most merely share ant habitats and have not been seen feeding on the ants. On the other hand, ant-mimicking spiders are infrequently found in mud-dauber nests as prey. Dr. W. S. Bristowe placed some British ant mimics together with six other spider species. Their ant-like movement and ant-like touch of the mimics' vibrating front legs made the spiders retreat, but the spiders were perfectly willing to eat dead ant mimics. So it appears that their ant-like look protects the mimics from at least some predators.

The differences between a typical spider and a typical ant are obvious. The ant has three body sections—head, thorax, and abdomen—while the spider has only two; spiders have eight legs and no antennas, while ants have six legs and a pair of constantly waving, probing antennas extending in front of their bodies; spiders tend to have rather plump bodies, while ants are elongated and slim. Ant-mimicking spiders, however, have long, slim bodies, and most carry their front legs up over the head, waving them about nervously as an ant waves its antennas. The second pair of legs reaches forward, giving the spider a six-legged look, and the spiders move with an ant-like jerky nervousness. Many ant-mimics have a constriction near the middle of the elongated cephalothorax and an elongated "waist" between the cephalothorax and the abdomen, giving the illusion of three body sections instead of two. One ant mimic in Montana uses a different method. When these spiders are medium-sized (these may all be males), they look like small

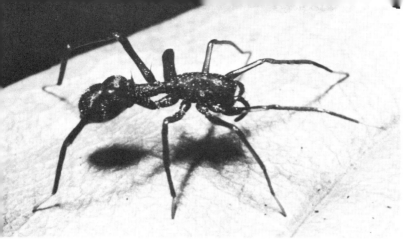

Many spiders look very much like ants. This resemblance probably protects them from their enemies. This spider from Panama, called Mazax pax, *is amazingly antlike in appearance. The front part of its abdomen is narrow like an ant's "waist." The end segments of its legs are light in color, making them more antlike in proportion to the body. The light ends of the front legs, combined with the darkened second-to-last segments, make them look like ant antennas held off the ground.* JONATHAN REISKIND

reddish-brown ants. The illusion of the head is provided by the enlarged pedipalps, which are rounded on the sides and held out in front, pressed together, to form a remarkably head-like illusion.

Many ant-mimics copy different ant species at different ages. In one running spider, the smallest individuals are black and shiny, like certain ants of similar size, while the larger but still immature spiders are yellow-orange and resemble larger ants. Adult females of this spider are dark brown and generally ant-like, while males are bright red-orange and look like entirely different ants.

One group of jumping spiders (genus Myrmarachne—"ant spider" in Greek) consists entirely of ant-mimicking species. Some of these spiders live in Africa, and Dr. Malcolm Edmunds has carefully studied three of them. Like the running spider species, the young of these salticids resemble certain ant species while the adults resemble others.

The spiders tend to inhabit the same sort of places as do their model ants. As the spiders grow, they can easily switch from association with one model to the other, either because the two species live near one another or because the ant copied by the young spider is especially common. Dr. Edmunds found that the spiders superficially copied the behavior as well as the appearance of the ants. With experience, however, he could see diffeernces. The spiders have a jerkier movement and turn their heads to look around. When alarmed, ants turn to defend themselves while the ant-mimicking spiders run and hide. This behavior probably gives the spider the best of both worlds. Its resemblance to the ants protects it from spider enemies, and its running away protects it from ant enemies.

Eleven
People and Spiders

Spiders are found everywhere people live, so it is no surprise that humans and spiders have interacted in many ways throughout history. It is a rare person who does not feel at least a bit uncomfortable in the presence of a large, dark, hairy spider darting across the floor. The feelings of discomfort, alarm, and fear which spiders stimulate seem to be related to several things—the spider's sudden, unpredictable movement, its hairiness, and its unexpected presence in the most private parts of our homes. The long, bent legs of the spider seem somehow threatening too. They make the animal appear to be much larger than it really is, and they give it an aggressive look, as if it were about to spring forward suddenly and attack.

Despite the human uneasiness about spiders, they have a prominent place in the mythologies of many peoples, often providing a link of one sort or another with the divine. The name "arachnid," used to include spiders and their relations, is derived from the name of a mythical Greek maiden who dared to challenge the gods. Arachne had a special talent for spinning and weaving. Not only were her creations beautiful, but the grace and charm of her technique made her beautiful to watch as she went about her work. Unfortunately, Arachne knew too well how talented she was, and challenged the goddess Athene, who invented spinning, to see which of them was better. Like any goddess, Athene was very angry at the conceit of a mere human who thought she could best a goddess. Athene gave Arachne one chance, appearing to her as an old woman and advising her that she should challenge other humans and should apologize to the goddess for her insolent behavior. Arachne was unmoved and merely repeated her challenge.

So the goddess and the maiden held their competition. Some stories say Athene became so angry that she broke Arachne's loom and beat her until Arachne hung herself. Other versions say that Athene won the contest and the maiden hung herself in despair over losing. In any case, after Arachne died, Athene decided to use her as an object lesson to those who would challenge the gods. She turned Arachne into a spider and condemned her to hang forever in her web on the thread she was weaving.

Spiders and Heroes

The spider as a friend comes through in some legends about this controversial creature. Religious stories tell that Jesus was saved from Herod's armies by a spider spinning a web across the entrance to the cave in which he was hiding, and there is a similar story about the Muslim leader Mohammed. The famous king of Prussia, Frederick the Great, was supposedly saved from an attempted poisoning by a spider which fell into a cup of tainted brew.

Legends sometimes tell us that we can learn something from spiders. Way back in the 14th century, the Scottish hero-king Robert the Bruce was hiding in a cave after disastrous battles with the English. While he pondered his fate, he happened to notice a spider attempting to attach a web-support thread across a corner of the ceiling. Six times the spider tried, and six times it failed. Robert watched and said, "Now shall the spider teach me what I am to do, for I also have failed six times." On its seventh attempt, the spider managed to span the distance successfully. Robert the Bruce left the cave full of confidence and determination, and went on to win his battle with the English.

Religion and Superstition

Probably because of the miraculous appearance of webs overnight and the mystery of their beauty, spiders have been considered as divine creatures, or as intermediaries between men and gods, in many religions. Among various peoples, including some South American and African tribes, a spider web is a sort of ladder to heaven, connecting the earthly and spiritual worlds. Among American Indians, the Dakota looked upon the orb web as a symbol of the heavens. The spiral was the origin of the power and mystery of the Great Spirit, and the four corners of the foundation lines represented the four directions from which the thunders came. In various Indian legends, an unfortunate human is able to escape from danger by lowering himself or herself on a rope of spider silk.

The Spider Woman is said by Navaho legend to have passed the secret of weaving to their tribe by way of a Pueblo girl who lived among them. The girl wandered away from the settlement and found a hole in the ground with smoke coming from it. Inside the hole was the Spider Woman spinning a web, and she invited the girl in. The Spider Woman welcomed the girl and passed on the secrets of weaving blankets and baskets to her over a period of several days. The girl took her new knowledge back to the Navahos and taught them to weave. Along with weaving came the warning from the Spider Woman that all weavers must leave a hole in the middle of each woven object or the Spider Woman would spin threads inside their heads. The hole represented the entrance to the Spider Woman's

burrow. Because of the demands for perfection by tourists, these holes are often cleverly disguised, but they may still be found in many Navaho blankets made today.

Good Luck and Bad

Human superstitions reveal our mixed-up feelings towards spiders. Black spiders, like black cats, are generally considered to be bad luck. But in Britain, tiny black spiders which make little silvery webs in meadows are called "money spiders" and are thought by some to bring money or other good fortune. Spiders are also believed by some to forecast the weather. Perhaps some of these ideas actually have some factual basis, for spiders may be able to perceive such clues as changes in air pressure. A sheet-web spider at the opening of its retreat, an orb web builder in the center of its web, and the building of an orb right after a rain storm are supposed to be signs of good weather. If an orb weaver shortens its lines, or if more spiders enter a house, bad weather is said to be on the way.

Almost everywhere, killing a spider is thought to bring bad luck. This belief may be due to the good-luck image of some spiders, or the mystically powerful reputation many spiders share, but various cultures have different explanations for it. West African folk tales portray spiders as having superior wisdom, while some natives of India believe that spiders received the spirits of their ancestors. Other peoples, like the Teton Indians, feared that the spirit of a dead spider would seek revenge upon its killer.

Spiders in Medicine

Many living things have been involved in medical practices through the ages, and spiders are no exception. Some old-time doctors and naturalists believed spiders to be good remedies for many ills. One such person was Dr. Thomas Muffet (1553–1609) whose daughter, Patience, earned everlasting fame for her own discomfort around spiders as "Little Miss Muffet." Unlike his daughter, Dr. Muffet enjoyed the company of spiders and admired the tapestries and hangings with which they decorated his home.

Dr. Muffet believed the spiders were good home remedies for most ills, noting that certain illnesses rarely occurred in houses where many spiders lived. He personally used many spider-based remedies. Perhaps his daughter's distaste for them arose because of these associations.

Since ancient times, spiders have had a reputation as relievers of fever. Until the 15th century, spiders were placed in nutshells or bags and hung around the neck to control fever. From the 16th century on, they were actually swallowed to achieve the desired effect. A Dr. Watson, in 1764, recommended, "Take a spider, alive, cover it with the new soft crummy Bread without bruising it; let the Patient swallow it fasting. This is an effectual cure, but many are set against it." Perhaps we can better sympathize with those "set against" it than with the doctor himself! Another doctor of the time realized that not everyone would be overjoyed at the idea of eating spiders, so he suggested giving the patient "a spider gently bruised and wrapped in a raisin or spread upon bread and butter."

Spider webs have had the reputation for stopping the flow of blood. This practice was first advocated during the first century A.D. Although there is no medical evidence that any component of the web has any effect on blood clotting, bits of web attached to a cut might provide a network of fibers upon which the blood clot could take shape more quickly.

Even today, black widow spider draglines, like the one shown here emerging from the spinnerets, are used to repair the crosshairs in old optical instruments. Notice the typical hourglass marking, which is red, on the underside of the abdomen. DR. R. F. FOELIX

Using Spider Silk

Many native peoples have used spider silk through the ages. The giant tropical spider Nephila makes golden webs over a meter (more than a yard) in diameter, with lines strong enough to trap small birds. New Guinea natives use this strong silk to make various kinds of nets for fishing as well as to weave caps, headdresses and bags. Australian aborigines make fishing lines from strands of Nephila webs. The body of the spider is crushed and rubbed over the ends of the line, and the body is tossed into the stream along with the fishing line. Small fish are attracted by the bits of spider, and when a fish tries to sample the tidbits clinging to the line, its tiny teeth become entangled in the web. Only small fish are caught this way, but many can be landed in a short time. Fish up to ⅓ kilogram (about ¾ pound) are supposed to be caught by this technique. Other kinds of spider web nets are used in other parts of the tropical Pacific.

Others have also tried to make use of spider silk, but with less success. In 1709, a Frenchman used silk from egg sacs to make some sample silk stockings and gloves. But after a flurry of excitement, practical considerations led to abandonment of the idea. In both Madagascar (now the Malagasy Republic) and the United States, ingenious men developed special "stocks" which held onto the spider while silk was reeled from its spinnerets. Dr. B. G. Wilder, in 1866, was able to get 138 meters (150 yards) from one spider. But even so, it would take 415 spiders to make less than a square meter (one square yard), and enough silk for a dress would use up 5,000 spiders.

Silkworms give more than twice as much silk as spiders and can be kept together crowded in cramped quarters. Spiders, on the other hand, are cannibals and must be separated from one another. Even the thickest spider silk is much finer than silkworm silk, so it is not as strong. Silkworm silk also makes a more lustrous cloth.

Spider silk, because it is so fine, has been used to make crosshairs in measuring instruments, telescopes, and gunsights. Up until World War I, spider silk was in some demand for this purpose. The dragline silk was usually used, and the joined fibers were separated to make single strands. The single strand averages only .000127 centimeters (1/20,000 inch) in diameter. Many different species were used, including various house spiders and black widows. Nowadays, tiny lines etched on glass or minute filaments of platinum or other metals are used for making crosshairs. But even today, black widows are kept at some military installations to help repair older optical instruments. When silk is desired, the spider is lifted onto a wooden wand over the floor, and she spins her way downward, producing the delicate silk used to fix up the old instruments.

Twelve
Learning about Spiders

With so many kinds of spiders living so close, spiders make perfect subjects for your own observations and science projects. Just by going outdoors at different times of day and hunting in different habitats, you can observe much about spider behavior. Gardens are especially good places to find spiders. Look carefully at flowers for white or yellow crab spiders, and separate the leaves of cabbages and broccoli for caterpillar-hunting spiders. Look between plants for orb webs. Observe which spiders build their webs in the morning and which in the evening. You can watch web-builders and hunters alike overwhelm their prey and note which kinds crush their prey as they feed and which merely suck them dry. If you are lucky, you may be able to observe spider courtship, too. By patiently waiting and watching, you can learn much about the lives of wild spiders. And since so many kinds have permanent homes, you can follow the daily activities of the same individuals for days or weeks.

Unfortunately, spider species are often not easy to identify, but you can get a good idea of what family a spider belongs to just by observing its web. The article, "Spiders and Webs," by E. L. Palmer (listed under "Suggested Reading"), can help you identify spiders by their webs. If you are interested in identifying spider species, *How to Know the Spiders* is a good guide to use.

Collecting Webs

If you like to collect things, spider webs provide a challenging subject for a collection, and you can gather your specimens without harming their creators one bit. To collect webs, you will need a supply of sturdy black or colored paper. Flocked paper (which has a roughened surface) is best. A can of white spray paint and one of clear lacquer are also needed. When you go out looking for webs, move towards the sun in the early morning or evening when the sun is low in the sky and the light will reflect off the web. Often in the early morning, dew drops decorating an orb will make it obvious as well as beautiful.

To collect the web, first scare off the spider so it will not be hurt by the paint and will be able to go make a new web. Hold the spray can about two feet from the web and spray evenly. Let that coat dry and spray again, laying on several coats to strengthen the web before cutting it. While the last coat is still slightly damp, bring a piece of paper carefully behind and press it against the web so it catches. Carefully cut any support threads which extend beyond the paper. If the web is not properly stuck to the paper at this point, it may collapse and be lost. It may take you awhile to perfect your technique. If you lose the web, try the same spot the next day. Chances are the spider will rebuild her web in the same place or nearby. Make notes about what sort of spider built the web, where you found it, and the time of day. After you have successfully collected the web on paper, spray it with a layer of clear lacquer for protection.

Spiders as Pets

Some spiders are quite easy to keep in jars or aquariums as pets. You can try to keep almost any spider you find as a pet by capturing it in a jar and punching small holes in the top or replacing the top with cheesecloth. A good way to catch a web-builder is to hold a jar directly beneath as you prod the spider gently with a stick. The spider should drop down on a dragline, right into your jar. Most spiders, except some which live in houses, will need a supply of water. Do not place a water dish in the container; the spider might drown in it. A bit of moistened sponge or cotton wool which is renewed every three days or so should be fine. Water can also be offered to larger spiders as a drop on the tip of an eyedropper. At first the spider will probably run away and hide if you offer it this way, but spiders can learn not to fear you and may learn to come right up and suck water from the dropper.

Hunting spiders will need sand or dirt in the bottom of their homes so they can move about, and they will need insects which do not fly as food. Mealworms, which are available in most pet stores, should work well. Web-spinnning spiders need some sort of framework for their webs. When we kept a black widow in a gallon jar, we gave her a few sticks to support her tangled web. You should not keep poisonous spiders as pets, but sticks would work well for any tangled-web weaver. Orb weavers need a web support such as an embroidery hoop or homemade frame which fits into the container. Flies make fine food for web-builders. If you have trouble finding flies, leave a container with some old cheese and coffee grounds on a windowsill with a light at night to attract some flies. Remember that spiders can do for quite awhile without food and can gorge themselves to store up for the future. As a rough guide for feeding, try offering your spider three or four insects about equal to it in weight each week. If your spider does not eat every time you feed it, do not worry. Just be patient and keep offering food. Maybe you will be lucky enough to see your

Some tarantulas make good pets and may become tame enough to hold on one's hand.

spider molt. Remember that most spiders have a short life-span and live only weeks or months before dying a natural death.

Tarantulas as Pets

By far the best spider pet is a tarantula. If you are careful to choose a female or immature male spider, you can keep your pet for many months or even years. Tarantulas are often sold in pet stores. Unfortunately, they are quite expensive. If you think you want a tarantula, try to get hold of *All About Tarantulas*, listed under Suggested Reading, before you buy your pet.

Tarantulas have very simple needs. A fish tank makes a fine home, if provided with a water dish, some sort of hideout like a flower pot on its side, and a covering of soil over the bottom. The cage must be covered, for tarantulas can climb glass. You must also be careful to keep the cage out of direct sunlight, or you could end up with a cooked spider. Tarantulas will eat grasshoppers, crickets, and smaller spiders. Fresh water should always be available to your pet. Many tarantulas are gentle enough to handle if you are careful, but you can also enjoy them if you leave them alone. American desert tarantulas make the best pets. Avoid buying the tropical kinds, which are more demanding, less gentle, and more expensive. Two common, hardy, and gentle kinds are called the "Mexican Brown" (*Aphonopelma smithi*) and the "Mexican Red-Leg" (*Dugesiella hentzi*) in pet stores.

If you do get hold of a tarantula, you may want to join the American Tarantula Society, which is composed of tarantula fans from across the country. The membership includes a subscription to their newsletter, *Tarantula Times,* a membership card, and a club badge. The address for more information is: American Tarantula Society, P.O. Box 2312, Bellingham, WA 98225.

Glossary

abdomen: Rear portion of the spider's body which contains most body organs. The spinnerets are on the abdomen.

arachnologist: A person who studies arachnids, a group which includes ticks, mites, scorpions, and other small arthropods, as well as spiders.

arthropod: An animal belonging to the Arthropoda, animals with an external skeleton and jointed legs, such as insects, crabs, spiders, etc.

ballooning: Drifting through the air using strands of silk; commonly done by spiderlings but sometimes also by adults of small spiders.

book lungs: Cavities filled with many folds of tissue where oxygen from the air can be extracted by the spider's blood. The book lungs are connected to the outside by small openings called spiracles.

cephalothorax: The front part of the spider's body, which consists of the head and thorax combined.

chelicerae: The first pair of appendages of the spider, which consist of a base piece and a hollow fang through which venom is injected into the prey.

cribellum: A flat, spinning plate located in front of the spinnerets of some spiders. The cribellum has many spigots through which very fine silk comes out.

cribellate spider: A spider with a cribellum.

cuticle: The exoskeleton—hard outer covering—of spiders and other arthropods.

ecribellate spider: A spider which lacks a cribellum.

hackled band: The tangled silk from the cribellum which is used to capture prey.

molting: Shedding the old cuticle, which is done several times during the spider's life; molting allows growth to occur.

mygale: Tarantula, trap-door spider, purse-web spider, or other "primitive" spider with chelicerae which swing forward and back rather than from side to side, and which have four book lungs.

palp: The end portion of the pedipalp; in male spiders it is modified into a reproductive organ.

pedipalps: The second appendages on the spider's head.

salticid: Member of the Salticidae, the jumping spiders.

spinnerets: Finger-shaped organs, studded with tiny pores and spigots through which the silk is spun.

spiracle: Openings in the abdomen leading to book lungs or tracheae.

tracheae: Air tubes penetrating body tissues; found in insects and some spiders.

Suggested Reading

Books

W. S. Bristowe, *The World of Spiders* (Taplinger, New York, 1976). Life histories of British spiders, well-written by a man who made a number of discoveries about spiders.

Willis J. Gertsch, *American Spiders*, Second Edition (Van Nostrand Reinhold, N.Y., 1979). Much information about spiders in general as well as chapters on American spiders, with many fine photos; not primarily a guide book.

Dale Lund, *All About Tarantulas* (TFH Publications, Neptune City, N.J., 1977). Small paperback with information about tarantulas and how to care for them.

Guide Books

B. J. Kaston, *How to Know the Spiders*, Third Edition (Wm. C. Brown, Dubuque, Iowa, 1978)

Herbert W. and Loran R. Levi, *Spiders and Their Kin* (Golden Guide Series, Western Publishing Co., Racine, WI, 1969)

Magazine Articles

R. E. Arnold, "Poison! Black Widow," *Field and Stream*, Oct. 1977

J. Wesley Burgess, "Social Spiders," *Scientific American*, March 1976

James H. Carmichael, Jr., "Jumping Spiders," *Natural History*, Oct. 1969

John A. L. Cooke, "Unveiling the Black Widow," *Natural History*, Feb. 1973

B. E. Dugdale, "The Weaving of an Engineering Masterpiece," *Natural History*, March 1969

William G. Eberhard, "Spider and Fly Play Cat and Mouse," *Natural History*, Jan. 1980

Howard E. Evans and Darryl T. Gwynne, "Jumping Spiders Is Their Name," *National Wildlife*, Jan-Feb 1980

J. B. Kaston, "Evolution of the Web," *Natural History*, April 1966

L. B. Lougee, "Amateur Scientist: How to Collect and Preserve Webs of Spiders," *Scientific American*, Feb. 1963

Ann Moreton, "Intrigue of the Web," *Audubon*, July 1972

E. L. Palmer, "Spiders and Webs," *Natural History*, Oct. 1961 Detailed description of common American spiders and their webs; good for identification.

Hans Pfletschinger, "Down Goes Aqua-Spider," *International Wildlife*, Jan-Feb 1980

Michael H. Robinson, "Wondrous Ways and Means of Tropical Spiders," *Smithsonian*, Oct. 1978

M. Romane, "Joys of Culturing Spiders and Investigating Their Webs," *Scientific American*, Dec. 1972

Theodore Savory, "Male Spider," *Natural History*, Nov. 1961

R. F. Sisson, "Spider That Lives Under Water," *National Geographic*, May 1972

Paul A. Zahl, "What's So Special About Spiders?" *National Geographic*, Aug. 1971

Index